CORPORATE GIRL
WELLNESS

CONTENTS

1 Preface

Welcome to the ultimate guide to mastering work-life wellness and becoming your best self! This is a roadmap to discovering your true aspirations, unlocking career success and bringing balance to your personal life. No matter where you are today, this guide is a reminder of your power to take charge and feel better today. Packed with transformative tools, practical strategies, and relatable real-life examples, we are here to help you rise above the pressures of the corporate world. Say goodbye to survival mode and step confidently into a space where thriving is inevitable!

Over the past 50 years, women have reshaped the corporate landscape, yet our advancements have come with unique challenges. We've had to adapt to systems originally designed by men, for men, often navigating environments that overlook our distinct strengths and perspectives. But as women, our potential is boundless; we're not limited to climbing the career ladder, running businesses, being life givers, homemakers, community leaders, or pioneers breaking down societal norms. We can be all of these, none of these, or anything we choose.

Too often, we're conditioned to believe that success demands relentless effort, that we must outwork everyone else, push ourselves to the brink, and equate exhaustion with achievement. It's a mindset that leaves us drained and unfulfilled. In today's hustle-driven world, it's easy to feel the weight of impossible expectations and it can often feel like we're somehow failing or falling behind the curve. The constant push to overachieve leaves little room to appreciate the progress we've already made, turning success into a moving target we're always chasing but never quite reaching.

This book challenges that narrative, showing you a new path where success and well-being go hand in hand. Offering a positive outlook and practical strategies to build the career and life you want, one that aligns with your core values. Whether you're aiming to climb the corporate ladder or simply carve out more "me time", this guide has everything you need to flourish. Discover a fresh perspective to excel in your career, enrich your daily life, and cultivate a deep sense of well-being. By prioritizing your wellness, you'll unlock a level of performance and success far beyond what stress and overwork could ever achieve.

The future you create will be nothing less than extraordinary.

2 Women have always worked

"I have ploughed and planted, and gathered into barns, and no man could head me. And ain't I a woman?" - Sojourner Truth

Women's history of work

Women have always worked. Throughout history, we have always worked, but our contributions to society often gone unrecognized and uncompensated. The story we are often told about how until the turn of the 20th century women were not allowed to work, is full of misinformation. In many societies, women were the backbone of family life, responsible for tasks essential to survival; gathering food, weaving, preserving food, cooking, child-rearing, and managing households.

These duties, often dismissed as "domestic chores," were in fact crucial to the well-being of families and communities. In addition, women have long been active in agriculture, small-scale trade, and cottage industries, contributing significantly to local economies. Despite the vital nature of their contributions, much of women's labour has been categorized as "invisible work," without acknowledgment in official histories or economic evaluations. The lack of formal recognition hasn't erased the fact that women's work has always been an engine driving economies.

Throughout history, many ancient societies, despite operating within patriarchal systems, saw women wield significant rights and influence. In ancient Egypt, for example, women enjoyed legal and economic autonomy far beyond what was common in other civilizations of the time. They could own and inherit property, negotiate contracts, and even represent themselves in court. Some ascended to the highest levels of power, ruling as pharaohs, while others held spiritual authority as priestesses. Their roles in governance, religion, and daily life underscore the remarkable agency and recognition afforded to women in Egyptian society.

In the world of Ancient Sparta, women were allowed to own and manage property. While men were away training or fighting, women played crucial roles in managing households and estates. Women's education in this society focused on physical fitness and intellectual development, aligning with the Spartan ideal of strong women producing strong warriors. Spartan girls underwent physical training, including running, wrestling, and throwing javelins, to ensure they were strong and healthy. These women were renowned for their influence in political and social matters, as noted by contemporary observers like Aristotle, who remarked on their prominence in Spartan society.

In Viking-age Scandinavia, women were also afforded many legal, social, and economic rights that were progressive for their time. Women could initiate divorce, and Norse law protected their property and dowry in such cases. This legal autonomy gave them significant control over their personal and economic lives. On top of this, their prominence is reflected in the Norse sagas, where women are often depicted as strategic thinkers, mediators, and leaders. Norse sagas and archaeological evidence suggest women participated in Viking expeditions, serving as settlers in colonized territories like Iceland, Greenland, and even Vinland (likely part of North America).

Evidence from the Viking Age indicates that women sometimes participated in warfare. One prominent example is the Birka Warrior, a high-status Viking burial discovered in Sweden. The grave, originally thought to belong to a man, was later identified as a woman through DNA analysis. She was buried with weapons and a full set of armour, suggesting her role as a warrior. Originally assumed to be a man, DNA analysis later confirmed the remains belonged to a woman buried with weapons and full armour, an indication of her status as a warrior.

Recent archaeological discoveries are dismantling long-held assumptions about rigid gender roles in the Palaeolithic era. A ground-breaking 2020 study uncovered the 9,000-year-old burial of a woman in Peru, buried alongside a set of hunting tools, challenging the belief that big-game hunting was solely a male pursuit. This suggests that women played an active role in hunting, reshaping our understanding of early human societies.

The artistic legacy of this period further underscores women's significance, with cave art and symbolic artefacts like the Venus figurines emphasizing their central place in cultural and spiritual life.

Fascinatingly, analysis of prehistoric handprints on cave walls suggests that many of these ancient masterpieces may have been created by women, offering a glimpse into their creative and influential presence in early human history.

These revelations paint a picture of ancient societies that were far more complex and inclusive than once thought, with women contributing to both survival and cultural expression in significant ways. This growing body of evidence is reshaping our understanding of gender roles in human history.

A warped view on our history

The word "spinster" may evoke outdated stereotypes today, but its medieval origins tell a tale of independence, resilience, and quiet defiance. In the Middle Ages, a spinster was simply a woman who spun wool or flax, a highly skilled and vital trade in pre-industrial societies. Spinning was more than just an occupation; it was a lifeline for many women, offering financial independence in an era when opportunities for self-sufficiency were rare.

Back then, being called a spinster was a mark of economic autonomy, not marital status. It was a title that recognized the important contributions of women who supported themselves and their communities through their craft. Yet over the centuries, the meaning shifted, unfairly burdened with negative connotations as societal norms around marriage and gender roles hardened.

This linguistic evolution obscures the empowering legacy of the spinster. In its original sense, it celebrated women who carved out lives on their own terms, challenging a world that often sought to limit their choices. The history of the word "spinster" is a reminder of how gender stereotypes have quietly formed and hacked away at our powerful past.

Similarly, the word "witch" once conjured images of wisdom and healing, embodying women who mastered herbal remedies and spiritual practices. These wise women were pillars of their communities, offering care and guidance in a time when such knowledge was indispensable. But by the late Middle Ages and early modern era, their influence became a target of fear and superstition.

Between the 15th and 17th centuries, the term "witch" transformed into a tool of persecution, wielded to silence independent, nonconforming women. Tens of thousands, often midwives, healers, or outspoken individuals, were accused, tortured, and executed during witch hunts. Midwives and healers, who held deep knowledge of natural remedies and women's health, were silenced, leaving gaps in medical understanding that would take centuries to reclaim.

Today, the story of the witch has taken on a new life. Feminist movements have reclaimed the title, celebrating its original associations with wisdom, resilience, and power. The "witch" now stands not as a figure of fear, but as a defiant symbol of female strength and autonomy.

Interestingly, modern "witches" often draw inspiration from historical practices, reviving herbalism and spiritual traditions that echo their ancestors' legacies.

The evolution of our right to equality

Women's rights and equality have fluctuated significantly across history, often influenced by changes in political, religious, and social systems. In ancient civilizations, before the understanding that men contributed to reproduction, women were often revered as powerful, almost divine beings due to their seemingly miraculous ability to create life. This led to the worship of female fertility and the elevation of goddesses associated with motherhood, agriculture, and the cycles of nature.

Matrilineal systems, where lineage and inheritance were traced through the mother, were common in many early cultures. This veneration, however, waned as scientific advancements and the realization of male involvement in conception shifted societal structures. As noted earlier, in ancient civilizations like the Roman Empire, women held many rights. While limited by patriarchal frameworks, these freedoms offered some degree of autonomy.

However, with the rise and institutionalization of early monotheistic religions, such as Christianity, these rights began to wane. As Christianity spread and solidified its power, women were increasingly marginalized, their roles in public and religious leadership diminished.

Notably, early Christian communities often revered women, with figures like Mary Magdalene and female deacons playing prominent roles. Yet, by the time the Church became a political force, patriarchal structures reasserted dominance, side-lining women from spheres of power and influence. Throughout history, religious teachings have often been used to justify women's subordination, with figures like St. Paul shaping interpretations that upheld patriarchal norms. This shift laid the foundation for centuries of systemic exclusion, demonstrating how ideological shifts can profoundly shape gender dynamics.

The relationship between monotheistic religions and women's rights is a tapestry of complexity. While these faiths are rooted in profound spiritual and ethical ideals, their interpretations over time have often contributed to legal and social restrictions on women. Yet, it's important to recognize that these limitations were less about the core beliefs of the religions themselves and more a reflection of cultural, political, and historical influences.

The political structures frequently selectively interpreted scriptures, using religion as a tool to entrench their authority, rather than reflecting the fundamental purpose or spirit of these faiths. The medieval period saw a further curtailing of women's freedoms, driven by the rise of feudalism and the dominance of the Catholic Church. Laws placed women under the control of men, relegating them to domestic roles and limiting their autonomy. The 16th-century Protestant Reformation deepened this patriarchal grip, reinforcing the idea that women's primary duties were to be obedient wives and mothers.

This systemic inequality was further cemented with the emergence of centralized states and codified laws. One glaring example is the Napoleonic Code of 1804, which stripped French women of key rights: they could no longer own property independently, vote, or initiate divorce. This legal framework went on to shape many other nations, embedding gender inequality into the very fabric of our modern legal systems.

As the 20th century dawned, a powerful shift began to take root. Women, no longer willing to accept the constraints of tradition, began to demand their rights, the right to vote, the right to education, and the freedom to shape their own futures. With an increasing number of women earning college degrees, they started to break free from the domestic sphere, venturing into professions like teaching, nursing, and secretarial work.

Then, the World Wars turned everything upside down. As men went off to fight, women stepped into roles once reserved for men, taking on leadership and industrial positions. After the wars, women re-entered the workforce in even greater numbers, though often relegated to lower-paying, lower-status jobs. But the 1960s and 1970s ignited a transformative wave of change.

The women's liberation movement surged forward, as women marched, rallied, and demanded equal rights in the workplace. They fought not just for equal pay, but for the opportunity to rise through the corporate ranks.

Landmark laws, like the Equal Pay Act of 1963 and Title VII of the Civil Rights Act of 1964, began to dismantle the barriers that had long kept women out of leadership, marking the beginning of a new era of empowerment and opportunity.

Despite these formidable barriers of our past, women have continually resisted and fought for their rights, laying the foundation for today's movements toward gender equality. Their enduring struggle is a testament to the resilience and determination that has shaped progress over centuries!

3 Women in todays' workplace

"We are here, not because we are law-breakers; we are here in our efforts to become law-makers."
— Emmeline Pankhurst.

The glass ceiling

The story of women entering the workforce as we know it today is a tale of relentless progress, driven by seismic social and economic changes. Before the 20th century, the idea of women in male-dominated roles was almost unthinkable. Society expected women to remain in the home, tending to domestic duties or working in low-paying, low-status jobs. Then the Industrial Revolution flipped the script.

As factories, offices, and industries boomed, women began to step out of the home and into the workforce in unprecedented numbers. While many were initially funnelled into clerical, secretarial, or factory roles, this marked the first major crack in the glass ceiling. Each job, no matter how humble, pushed the boundaries of what was deemed acceptable for women, setting the stage for the larger, bolder strides that would follow in the coming decades.

Caroline Haslett was a visionary leader of this era, who electrified women's roles in industry and technology. In 1924, she co-founded the Electrical Association for Women (EAW), the first organization of its kind dedicated to educating women on electricity. Haslett believed that electrification could liberate women from time-consuming domestic chores, empowering them to enter the workforce and pursue technical professions. Haslett's influence extended globally as she became the first female member of the prestigious Institute of Electrical Engineers.

During World War I and II, women had been called upon to fill roles traditionally held by men who were off fighting, including positions in factories, offices, and even in the armed forces. As women took on these jobs, they proved not only their capability but also their value to the economy and the workforce. Women were not just supporting the war effort from home during World War II, they were at its very heart, contributing directly to military service.

Dame Vera Laughton Mathews emerged as a ground-breaking leader in this movement, taking the helm as Director of the Women's Royal Naval Service (WRNS). Mathews led the charge to break down traditional gender barriers, assigning women to vital roles such as coding, radar operation, and communications, jobs that were crucial for the Royal Navy's success. Her leadership marked a pivotal moment in the acknowledgment of women's extraordinary contributions to wartime efforts.

The post-war period marked a crucial turning point, as women's participation in the workforce expanded and their fight for equality in the workplace gained momentum. While many women returned to domestic life after the war, the workforce never looked the same. By 1951, women made up over 30% of the UK workforce, thriving in sectors such as textiles, teaching, and healthcare. These steps, small but significant, helped redefine what was possible for women and ignited the flame of gender equality.

Our place today

Today, women are not just participants in the corporate landscape, they are catalysts for transformation. By spearheading innovation, fostering inclusive cultures, and propelling companies toward ground-breaking success, women are redefining what it means to lead. Our leadership brings fresh perspectives and critical insights that elevate decision-making and problem-solving to new heights.

The 2020 "Diversity Wins: How Inclusion Matters" report revealed that companies with the highest levels of gender diversity on executive teams were around 25% more likely to see above-average profitability, compared to those with less diverse leadership. Examining data from over 1,000 large companies across 15 countries, the study underscored the powerful correlation between diverse leadership and financial performance.

By 2023, women made up nearly half of the U.S. labour force and held around 40% of managerial positions globally, a remarkable achievement that underscores our growing influence in the workplace. Yet, despite these gains, significant barriers remain. Women continue to be underrepresented at the highest levels, with only around 10% of executive roles in S&P 500 companies held by women. This disparity highlights the work still to be done, but it also signals a powerful potential for future change.

Female founders have reshaped industries and built some of the world's most ground-breaking businesses, often overcoming incredible challenges along the way. Sara Blakely, the visionary behind Spanx, revolutionized the shapewear industry with a simple yet innovative idea. With just $5,000 in savings, Blakely crafted a product that redefined comfort and confidence in women's clothing. Her relentless drive and ingenuity propelled her into billionaire status, demonstrating that with vision and perseverance, barriers can be shattered.

Then there's Whitney Wolfe Herd, the founder of Bumble, who transformed the world of online dating by creating a platform that empowers women to make the first move. Her focus on inclusivity and safety catapulted Bumble to international success, making her the youngest self-made female billionaire following its IPO. These women, and countless others, have built thriving businesses by identifying gaps in their industries and pushing relentlessly toward their goals.

Their stories prove that determination, creativity, and resilience are the ultimate drivers of entrepreneurial success, turning bold ideas into global empires. Women are proving that leadership isn't just about authority, it's about connection, collaboration, and creating a space where everyone thrives. Women are not just boosting the bottom line, they are transforming the very culture of the workplace.

With a unique focus on emotional intelligence, women are championing empathy, active listening, and a deeper understanding of the organisation's heartbeat. Gone are the days of top-down, authoritarian leadership. Women are leading with collaboration at the forefront, promoting teamwork and inclusivity. This leadership style fosters innovation, sparks creativity, and builds stronger connections, allowing everyone to feel seen and valued.

The female experience in the workplace

Women have broken into a corporate world long dominated by men, yet the echoes of this historical imbalance still shape their experiences today. Many women find themselves facing a steeper climb up the corporate ladder, with harder battles for promotions and recognition. Despite their achievements, they often have to prove themselves more, navigating an environment where their contributions can be overlooked or undervalued.

Moreover, many continue to endure the pervasive threat of sexual harassment, microaggressions and general sexist attitudes, a harsh reminder of the challenges that remain. Despite recent measures to protect women through workplace policies, harassment can still thrive due to power dynamics and cultural norms. The struggle for equality in the workplace is far from over, and women are still pushing against the systemic obstacles that hinder their full participation and advancement.

A universal experience that many women face as a result of the steeper climb in the workplace is the overwhelming weight of burnout. Constantly pushing to prove their worth, women often find themselves stretched thin, balancing demanding workloads, navigating biases, and striving for advancement, all while managing the expectations of both their professional and personal lives. The relentless pressure to do more, be more, can leave them feeling depleted, exhausted, and mentally drained.

According to a study by Gallop, women are more likely to experience burnout. This heightened risk is linked to the dual pressures of professional demands and domestic responsibilities. Additionally, a survey by the Women's Health Foundation reveals that around 70% of working women felt overwhelmed by their workload, and many say they have experienced symptoms of burnout. These figures underscore the urgent need for effective strategies and support systems to address and promote well-being.

Why are so many women experiencing burnout and facing constant challenges in the workplace? The answer often lies in the overwhelming juggling act we're expected to perform, balancing demanding careers with the responsibilities at home. The stress of trying to excel in both areas can quickly pile up, leaving little room for rest or self-care. Add to that the lack of flexible work options, whether it's reasonable parental leave or the ability to adjust work hours, and the struggle becomes even more difficult.

On top of this, women in male-dominated industries, often face the unspoken pressure to prove themselves constantly, pushing them to go above and beyond just to be seen or taken seriously. As a result, many women feel they must work twice as hard to earn the same recognition or opportunities as their male counterparts. On top of that, women are often expected to take on additional roles in the workplace, such as mentoring or handling "office housework" like organizing events, all without extra compensation or recognition.

On top of all these challenges, women are frequently asked to fit into a mould that wasn't designed with us in mind. There's little room to embrace our unique traits or align with our energy cycles. Instead, we're often pushed to lean into more traditionally masculine qualities and work styles. This pressure to conform to a standard that doesn't cater to our nature can be exhausting and deeply frustrating over time, leaving little space for us to thrive in the workplace.

Well-being in the workplace

With the rise of trends like the "soft girl era" and a growing movement that champions a return to femininity, the question becomes even more relevant: how can we carve out time for leisure, enjoyment, and self-care while still navigating the demands of a fast-paced workplace and the high expectations of the "female boss" lifestyle? Balancing these two worlds, embracing our true selves while navigating the pressures of professional success, requires a shift in both personal mindset and organizational culture. It's about finding harmony between ambition and rest, power and softness, and ultimately, creating space for women to thrive authentically in all aspects of their lives.

4 Barriers and challenges

"A woman with a voice is, by definition, a strong woman. But the search to find that voice can be remarkably difficult." – Melinda Gates

The uphill battle

Significant strides have been made in recent decades to reduce barriers for women in the workplace, leading to more equitable environments. Legislation such as the Equal Pay Act has been pivotal in addressing wage disparities and promoting gender equality. Equal pay rights have evolved from a fringe concern to a global issue, underscoring the long-standing struggle for true economic equality. Organizations have increasingly adopted policies that support work-life balance, such as flexible working hours and parental leave, acknowledging the dual responsibilities many women juggle.

Advancements in understanding the science of women's bodies and their unique needs have played a transformative role in making the modern workplace more inclusive for women. Research into ergonomics, reproductive health, and workplace stress has revealed critical insights that can shape future policies and practices.

These advancements reflect a growing recognition of the value women bring to the workplace and a commitment to fostering an environment where everyone has the opportunity to succeed.

In today's corporate landscape, women continue to face numerous challenges that are deeply rooted in a history of workplaces designed with only men in mind. These challenges are multifaceted, encompassing both structural and biological aspects that can significantly impact a woman's career trajectory and overall well-being. The traditional corporate workplace was conceived at a time when societal norms dictated that men were the primary breadwinners and women were caregivers.

This history led to workplace policies that inadequately support work-life balance, particularly for women who still bear a disproportionate share of family responsibilities. Insufficient parental leave, inflexible work hours, and a lack of affordable childcare options are just a few examples of how outdated corporate structures fail to accommodate the modern working woman. As a result, women often face an untenable choice between their careers and their personal lives.

Pregnancy and the postpartum period introduce specific needs that are often neglected in corporate policies. Women require accommodations such as more frequent breaks, access to maternity leave, and private spaces for breastfeeding or pumping milk. Unfortunately, many workplaces lack these essential facilities, creating significant stress for women who are forced to choose between their health, their family's well-being, and their careers. The stress of navigating a corporate environment that does not cater to our needs can have a profound impact on women's health. Women are more susceptible to stress-related conditions such as anxiety, depression, and autoimmune disorders. The dual demands of work and family life, coupled with a lack of corporate support for stress management, can exacerbate these conditions, leading to long-term health consequences.

The persistent gender pay gap and financial literacy

The gender pay gap remains a stark reminder of the inequities within corporate compensation structures. Even when women perform the same roles as their male counterparts, they are often paid less. This disparity is perpetuated by opaque pay structures and negotiation processes that disadvantage women. When women are consistently paid less, it perpetuates the perception that their work is less valuable, impacting their chances of being considered for promotions. Despite efforts to close the gap, it remains a significant barrier to true gender equality in the workplace.

The cumulative financial impact of the pay gap means women save less for the future, invest less in personal growth, and are often less financially secure. In the long-run, this translates into fewer resources and capital to take risks, such as starting a business or taking on new career path, which can hinder their potential to succeed. Historically, women have faced significant barriers to accessing education on managing finances and investing, benefits that were reserved only for men.

This lack of access left many women unprepared to manage their finances or invest for the future, contributing to long-term wealth gaps between genders. While progress has been made with the rise of financial education programs aimed at women, the historical disparities in financial literacy continue to echo in modern economic inequalities.

Lack of Mentorship and Sponsorship

A significant hurdle woman encounter in the corporate world is the absence of robust mentorship and sponsorship networks. Historically dominated by men, these networks often excluded women, whether intentionally or unintentionally, leaving them without critical guidance or advocacy for career advancement. Studies show that professionals with sponsors are more likely to progress in their careers, yet only one in five women reports having a sponsor.

Male-exclusive networks can unknowingly reinforce unconscious biases, creating environments where individuals with similar experiences or backgrounds are prioritized. This often leads to male colleagues being favoured for promotions or leadership roles, simply because they share common connections. As a result, women are often left out of critical conversations, opportunities, and mentorship that could propel their careers forward. This reinforces the panes of the glass ceiling and slows progress toward gender equity in leadership.

Mentorship plays a pivotal role in helping individuals build skills, navigate corporate culture, and gain insights into career strategies. Sponsorship goes a step further: it involves influential leaders using their positions to actively advocate for their protégés, opening doors to opportunities that might otherwise remain out of reach. Without access to these networks, women are often left to navigate their careers without the support and advocacy essential for upward mobility.

Work Hours and Productivity Cycles

Traditional corporate work hours, with their rigid structure, often fail to align with the natural rhythms of women's bodies, overlooking the unique health needs that fluctuate throughout their life stages. Research shows that women's cognitive performance varies with hormonal cycles, such as higher focus and verbal fluency during the follicular phase and enhanced creativity and problem-solving abilities during the luteal phase. A standard, one-size-fits-all work schedule disregards these natural shifts, which can hinder productivity and innovation.

For women navigating significant life changes, like pregnancy, postpartum recovery, or menopause, the challenges are even more pronounced. Pregnancy often brings fatigue, morning sickness, and other health concerns that are not accommodated by rigid work hours. Postpartum women frequently struggle to balance demanding jobs with sleep deprivation and caregiving duties, while menopause symptoms such as hot flashes, insomnia, and mood swings remain largely ignored in workplace wellness discussions.

Additionally, corporate schedules tend to neglect women's reproductive health needs, such as menstrual pain, fertility treatments, or conditions like endometriosis. These issues require flexibility and understanding, things that many workplaces fail to provide. Without proper accommodations, women face added burdens, making it difficult to juggle both their health and professional responsibilities. Jobs that demand prolonged sitting or standing without adequate breaks can also increase risks during pregnancy, such as swelling, varicose veins, or even preterm labour.

For women, a work environment that doesn't recognize these unique needs only compounds the challenge of maintaining health and thriving professionally. This disconnect between traditional work structures and women's natural rhythms doesn't just impact productivity, it can also lead to increased stress, burnout, and attrition.

Flexible schedules, remote work options, and wellness-focused policies can help bridge the gap, fostering a healthier and more inclusive workplace for everyone.

Physical Workspace Design

Corporate environments are often designed with a one-size-fits-all approach that primarily caters to the male body. In the book *Invisible Women*, Caroline Criado Perez exposes the systemic bias that leaves women overlooked in a world designed around male physiology. The book reveals how corporate environments, from office layouts to medical research and technology, fail to account for the differences between male and female anatomy. Perez uncovers issues like gender-biased ergonomics, temperature settings, and the lack of female representation in data, all of which contribute to discomfort and inequality for women.

Even as we walk into our office building, the temperatures are typically set based on the male metabolic rate, making workplaces uncomfortably cold for many women's natural body temperatures. Research shows that women generally feel more comfortable at higher temperatures, yet this is rarely considered in the ergonomics of an office set-up.

Similarly, standard office furniture is often designed for male body measurements, leading to poor posture, musculoskeletal pain, and conditions like carpal tunnel syndrome.

Desks and chairs that don't fit the female frame can cause strain on the back, neck, and shoulders, and ergonomic mismatches worsen the physical toll. Women are sacrificing their health just to hold a seat at table, literally and metaphorically.

These physical misalignments not only affect women's well-being but also their productivity. Discomfort and health problems resulting from poorly designed workspaces can lead to mental fatigue. The constant effort to maintain comfort in an unsuitable environment can also contribute to stress, further impacting mental and physical health. Over time, this can lead to decreased job performance, increased absenteeism, and long-term health issues that require medical intervention.

To address these challenges, workplaces must embrace inclusive design; adjustable desks, ergonomic chairs, and customizable temperature controls are essential. By prioritizing these changes, companies can improve employee health, enhance performance, and create a more equitable, productive environment for all.

Successes championed by women

Despite the barriers, women in the workplace are making significant progress in improving conditions for wellness in the workplace. Women in leadership are pushing for policies that promote work-life balance. This drive for balance isn't just about accommodating personal needs but about cultivating a workplace culture that values well-being and prevents burnout.

Women often prioritize transparent communication, encouraging dialogue across all levels of the company. This creates trust and empowers employees to speak up and contribute their ideas. By embracing these typically feminine traits; empathy, collaboration, mentorship, and holistic thinking, women are redefining success in the workplace.

Women are at the forefront of transformative changes in the workplace. Sheryl Sandberg, the COO of Meta (formerly Facebook), stands out as a powerful advocate for women in leadership and work-life balance. Her Lean In movement and best-selling book, Lean In: Women, Work, and the Will to Lead, have inspired countless women to pursue leadership roles while urging companies to create more equitable and supportive environments for working parents. Sandberg's influence has sparked conversations and tangible changes in how organizations empower women in the workplace.

Within the corporate sphere, leaders like Cindy Robbins have set bold examples. As the former president and chief people officer of Salesforce, Robbins led a critical internal audit in 2015 that exposed concerning gender pay disparities. She championed a $3 million commitment to close the gap and established annual audits to ensure continued pay equity.

Robbins' actions have encouraged other major companies to follow suit, raising the bar for accountability in corporate America.

Patagonia's former CEO, Rose Marcario, redefined what it means to lead with purpose. Under her leadership, Patagonia became a global model for corporate social responsibility, prioritizing environmental sustainability and fair labour practices. Marcario's vision set new standards for ethical business operations and demonstrated the powerful impact of aligning corporate success with positive social impact.

On the global stage, Iceland made history in 2018 by becoming the first country to mandate equal pay by law, requiring companies to prove they pay men and women equally. Activists like Hanna Birna Kristjánsdóttir, a former minister of the interior, and Vigdís Finnbogadóttir, the world's first democratically elected female head of state, were instrumental in driving this landmark legislation. Their trailblazing efforts have inspired other nations to confront and address pay disparities.

These women, through their leadership and advocacy, have left lasting legacies, proving that transformative change is not only possible but essential in building a more inclusive and equitable workplace.

Successes championed by men

Focusing on the positive is a powerful catalyst for meaningful change. History shows that some of the most significant strides in women's rights were achieved through collective efforts, with men and women joining forces to challenge societal norms. Male allies, in particular, have often played pivotal roles in advancing equality, proving that progress thrives on collaboration.

One trailblazer in this regard was John Stuart Mill, the 19th-century British philosopher and economist. Far ahead of his time, Mill championed women's rights with conviction, particularly in his revolutionary work, The Subjection of Women (1869). He argued that true equality hinged on women's ability to work, earn fair wages, and fully participate in society, including securing the right to vote. As a Member of Parliament, Mill became a pioneer for women's suffrage, proposing it formally in 1866, a daring move that ignited public debate.

He believed that economic independence for women was not just a moral imperative but a necessity for societal progress, as denying equal opportunities squandered half of humanity's potential. His feminist philosophy was deeply influenced by his wife, Harriet Taylor Mill, whose intellectual partnership helped shape his ground-breaking ideas. Together, they demonstrated how collaboration amplifies the fight for justice, setting an enduring example of ally-ship.

In the United States, Franklin D. Roosevelt made his mark as an unexpected ally for women's workplace inclusion during his presidency. Amid the twin crises of the Great Depression and World War II, Roosevelt's New Deal programs created millions of jobs, including roles for women through initiatives like the Works Progress Administration (WPA). During WWII, Roosevelt encouraged women to enter traditionally male-dominated industries, symbolized by the cultural icon "Rosie the Riveter." This shift not only bolstered the war effort but also challenged entrenched gender norms.

Another decisive moment came in 1920 when Harry T. Burn, a young legislator from Tennessee, cast the vote that ratified the 19th Amendment, granting women the right to vote. Influenced by a heartfelt letter from his mother urging him to "do the right thing," Burn's bold decision exemplifies how individual actions can ripple through history, reinforcing women's roles in both democracy and the workplace.

Fast-forward to today, and the spirit of male ally-ship continues through global campaigns like UN Women's HeForShe. Launched in 2014, the initiative has mobilized men worldwide to advocate for gender equality across all sectors. Notable champions include former U.S. President Barack Obama, a vocal advocate for equal pay and workplace opportunities, and Canadian Prime Minister Justin Trudeau, who proudly identifies as a feminist and champions gender parity in leadership.

Their actions underscore an enduring truth: true equality requires a shared effort from both genders. These examples remind us that progress often stems from collaboration. When men advocate for equality, they not only support women but also help dismantle systemic barriers, creating a more inclusive and prosperous world for everyone, including for themselves.

5 Benefits of the modern era

"The biggest shift in the modern workplace is the recognition that well-being and productivity are connected.
– Ariana Huffington

In good condition

The evolution of the modern workplace over the past century is a story of dramatic transformation, from harsh, exploitative conditions to the more structured and increasingly inclusive environment we recognize today. At the turn of the 20th century, work was gruelling and often dehumanizing. The Industrial Revolution had reshaped economies and societies, but it came with a cost.

Workers, including women and children, endured long hours in unsafe conditions for meagre wages. It was not uncommon for workers to clock more than 60 hours a week with little job security or legal protections. The concept of "work-life balance" was virtually non-existent, and the expectations for women were clear. Once married or with children, women were expected to leave the workforce.

The end of World War II ushered in a period of seismic change, marking the dawn of a new corporate era. The economic boom of the 1950s sparked a rapid expansion of corporations.

Companies grew, establishing distinct departments, specialized roles, and a tier of middle management. At the same time, the post-war labour rights movements, fuelled by decades of activism, began to achieve significant victories. Laws were enacted to guarantee a 40-hour workweek and establish minimum wage standards, providing greater protections for workers.

Yet, despite these monumental changes, the workplace remained overwhelmingly male-dominated. Women continued to fight for equal opportunities, battling lower wages and systematic exclusion from leadership positions. Empowered by the feminist movements of the 1960s and 1970s, more women began to enter higher education and professional fields, though significant disparities remained.

The late 20th century witnessed the onset of the digital revolution, forever altering the landscape of work. The rise of personal computers, the internet, and other technologies boosted efficiency and automated many manual tasks. Meanwhile, globalization was reshaping the workforce, demanding new skills and driving greater diversity into workplaces.

At the same time, corporate culture began evolving toward greater flexibility, with work-life balance gaining traction and companies offering benefits like flexible hours and wellness programs.

A change in society's mindset

It's important to acknowledge the shift in this generation's mindset plays a significant role in how the modern workplace has much improved. The generational mindset around existing just to work had undergone a profound shift. In the past, hard work was often equated with long hours, physical labour, and a relentless drive, where burnout was worn as a badge of honour. Today's generation is redefining what success truly means, placing a stronger emphasis on mental health, balance, and sustainability.

There's growing recognition that success isn't just about climbing the corporate ladder, it's about flourishing in all areas of life. People are realizing that productivity and happiness aren't mutually exclusive; in fact, they're deeply intertwined. This generation is embracing the idea that well-being is essential to professional success. The narrative has shifted from "work hard at all costs" to "work smarter, prioritize self-care, and find balance." This holistic approach signals a profound cultural shift, where success is measured not just by achievements, but by how well we nurture our minds, bodies, and relationships along the way.

The modern workplace has undergone a remarkable transformation, thanks to advancements in technology. Innovations like cloud computing, video conferencing, and automation have revolutionized the way we work, making remote work both feasible and widely accepted. The COVID-19 pandemic only accelerated this shift, solidifying remote and hybrid work models as the new norm.

Alongside these changes, there's been a significant push for diversity, equity, and inclusion (DEI), with companies implementing policies to ensure fair practices for underrepresented groups.

A standout improvement in today's workplace is the emphasis on employee well-being and flexibility. Flexible work arrangements, including remote work, flexible hours, and compressed workweeks, allow employees to achieve a better balance between their professional and personal lives. Wellness programs focusing on mental, physical, and emotional health are widespread, contributing to a more supportive work environment. Additionally, companies are increasingly offering benefits that accommodate various life stages, such as parental leave and elder care support, recognizing the importance of our personal lives outside of work.

This evolving landscape has created a more inclusive environment, with networks, mentorship opportunities, and resources designed to help women thrive. Gender equality has made significant strides, with more women in leadership roles, better pay, and policies that support career advancement. Today's workplaces have shifted from rigid, demanding environments to ones that foster a culture of support and empowerment, where employees feel more valued.

Physical health

Before industrialization, work was closely aligned with the rhythms of nature. In agrarian societies, farmers worked long hours during planting and harvest seasons, but enjoyed more downtime during the winter. However, the Industrial Revolution radically transformed the landscape of work. Factories demanded continuous production, leading to gruelling workdays of 12 to 16 hours, six days a week. Child labour was rampant, and breaks were scarce. Rest and holidays became rare luxuries, as factory owners prioritized maximizing output above all else.

The harsh realities of the Industrial Age eventually sparked labour movements in Europe and North America. In 1842, British textile workers won a landmark case limiting child labour hours, and the movement for shorter workdays gained momentum. By the 1860s, American workers were demanding "Eight hours for work, eight hours for rest, and eight hours for what we will," pushing for the eight-hour workday we know today.

Fast forward, and the modern workplace looks drastically different. While physically demanding jobs in industries like construction and agriculture continue to pose health risks such as musculoskeletal injuries and chronic pain, the shift toward knowledge-based work has allowed for significant improvements. Office jobs, which often involve less physical strain, have made it easier for individuals of all physical abilities to thrive in the workforce, regardless of age or life stage. The physical toll is much lower in modern office roles, allowing for longer, more sustainable careers.

In contrast to the manual labour of the past, which often led to early retirement due to physical exhaustion and wear-and-tear on joints, today's knowledge-based jobs allow individuals to remain in the workforce longer, with fewer physical risks. The rise of flexible work arrangements, greater focus on wellness, and a more supportive environment have further improved the modern workplace, offering opportunities for work-life balance and long-term career growth without the debilitating physical demands of earlier industrial jobs.

More interesting roles

The modern workplace has blossomed into an ecosystem filled with roles that are more exciting and versatile than ever before. Driven by rapid technological advances, globalization, and evolving societal values, entirely new fields have emerged, reshaping the concept of a career. A century ago, jobs like "AI specialist" or "digital marketer" would have seemed like something out of a sci-fi novel. Careers in sustainability consulting are now at the forefront of tackling the global climate crisis, while breakthroughs in biotechnology are revolutionizing healthcare and agriculture.

The rise of the gig economy and remote work has shattered the traditional office model, offering people the freedom to work from anywhere, whether it's a beach in Bali or a cosy Scandinavian home office. Unlike the repetitive, rigid roles of the industrial era, today's jobs demand creativity, adaptability, and the ability to blend diverse fields of knowledge. In fact, studies predict that around 80% of the jobs that will exist by 2030 haven't even been invented yet, illustrating the rapid pace at which the workplace is evolving. This new era of work is not just about earning a pay-check; it's about making a meaningful impact and shaping the future.

Automation and technology have eliminated many mundane tasks, allowing workers to focus on more engaging, high-value activities. For instance, instead of manually sorting data, today's professionals use advanced software to analyse trends and drive business strategy. Marketing teams have moved beyond basic ads, leveraging data analytics and behavioural psychology to craft sophisticated, global campaigns. Human resources, once an administrative function, has transformed into a proactive force driving organizational development, diversity, and employee engagement.

Financial analysts now use predictive algorithms to forecast market trends, while UX designers blend psychology with design principles to create intuitive digital experiences. These changes highlight how the corporate world is embracing roles that require critical thinking, creativity, and a deep understanding of complex systems, leaving behind the drudgery of repetitive tasks in favour of innovation and strategic impact. This intellectual shift has made modern roles not just more rewarding, but also more impactful.

Education opportunities

Employers today are increasingly invested in the development of their teams, offering opportunities for employees to pursue new courses, certifications, and qualifications. From paid training programs and leadership courses to full reimbursement for higher education, these initiatives are transforming careers and enabling workers to stay ahead of the curve in an ever-evolving job market. But it doesn't stop at traditional education.

Many companies are embracing innovative learning models by partnering with professional development organizations or online platforms to provide employees with tailored courses designed to boost critical skills. Whether it's mastering the latest technology, improving communication techniques, or building expertise in areas like data analytics or project management, these programs empower employees to broaden their qualifications and open doors to new career possibilities.

For many employees, their workplace has become a gateway to opportunities they never had when leaving school, including access to university-level education. By covering tuition costs and often providing flexible work arrangements to accommodate study schedules, employers are empowering individuals to earn qualifications that once seemed out of reach. For these employees, their job becomes more than just a source of income; it's a second chance to achieve educational goals, elevate their career prospects, and unlock their potential.

This investment not only enriches the lives of workers but also strengthens companies with a more skilled and motivated workforce. Ultimately, investing in continuous learning creates a win-win scenario. Employees become more adaptable, innovative, and skilled, driving the company's success while simultaneously enhancing their own career prospects.

In a job market that's increasingly competitive, companies offering these opportunities are not just attracting top talent, they're building a workforce that is future-ready, poised to thrive in the face of new challenges and opportunities.

Financial security

In the past, financial security for the working class was far from guaranteed, with workers often facing precarious conditions. While social structures and traditions provided some stability, many employees were paid low wages for long hours, with little job security or bargaining power. With no formal contracts or employment protections, many workers faced temporary employment, frequent layoffs, and no safety nets like unemployment benefits.

Losing a job meant immediate financial hardship, leaving workers vulnerable and exposed. On top of that, injuries sustained on the job were often seen as the worker's responsibility, with no compensation or medical coverage to support their recovery.

This lack of financial protection and safety net not only made it harder to bounce back but also intensified the stress of navigating an unpredictable labour market.

Today, the modern workplace offers a far more stable financial landscape. Employment contracts have become standardized, with laws introducing minimum wage, paid sick leave, and guaranteed benefits. Corporations now offer competitive salaries, bonuses, and regular pay raises, contributing to income stability. Employees often enjoy comprehensive benefits like health insurance, retirement plans, paid vacations, and even stock options. Additionally, many companies offer career progression pathways, well-established HR policies, and severance packages, reducing economic uncertainty and offering a financial safety net.

Being employed in today's corporate environment can minimise a significant number of stressors from your daily life. A freelancer or business owner will tell you that while the freedom of running your own show is undeniably appealing, it often comes with the downside of not having a regular, stable income. The allure of being your own boss and having control over your schedule is tempting, but the reality can be far more daunting than anticipated.

Freelancing or owning a business demands immense sacrifice, and the constant hustle can blur the lines between work and personal life, leaving little room to recharge. The pressure to succeed, coupled with the financial uncertainty that comes with irregular income, can feel overwhelming, even for the most passionate and driven entrepreneurs.

By contrast, a steady pay-check provides a sense of stability, minimizing immediate financial risks and offering peace of mind in your day to day.

That doesn't mean the corporate world is suitable for everyone. For many, it serves as a valuable stepping stone toward entrepreneurial dreams or financial independence. With the security and resources provided by your current role, you can craft a clear path to your goals, whether that's building a business, climbing in your career or pursuing other life ambitions, without sacrificing financial stability or peace of mind.

6 Why we often face burnout

"Sometimes, you have to let go of the life you planned, so as to embrace the one that is waiting for you." — Joseph Campbell

Finding your place

Before we dive into the strategies for reviving your joy at work and transforming your daily routine, it's essential to acknowledge something many of us experience: burnout. If you're in a corporate job, you're not alone in feeling drained and overwhelmed, it's a struggle that's all too common in today's fast-paced, high-pressure work environments. Considering all the challenges we've discussed in the previous chapters, it's completely natural to often feel like a fish out of water.

Feeling out of place or unable to thrive doesn't mean you lack intelligence, capability, or potential. Often, it's a sign that you're adapting to an unfamiliar environment or that your current role doesn't align with your true strengths and passions. Growth isn't about forcing yourself to fit, it's about finding where you naturally shine. Even though there have been significant strides in improving workplace conditions, burnout continues to be a major issue in corporate jobs, and it often stems from a few key challenges.

One of the biggest culprits is the constant pressure to perform at a high level, with technology keeping us always "on" and accessible, making it hard to fully disconnect. The lines between work and personal life have become increasingly blurred, especially with the rise of remote work. On top of that, the never-ending demands of multitasking and an information overload can leave us feeling stretched too thin. When employees lack control over their schedules or workloads, exhaustion and stress quickly set in. Despite the perks of the modern workplace, the unrealistic expectations, weak boundaries, and the difficulty of truly "switching off", still leave many of us feeling overwhelmed.

At work, feeling like a "fish out of water" often happens when you're thrown into a new role, team, or company culture that feels drastically different from what you're used to. You might find yourself struggling to adjust to new expectations, unfamiliar processes, or a team dynamic that doesn't align with your strengths or values. Whether it's being the new hire, taking on a leadership role for the first time, or adapting to new technology, this sense of being out of place can lead to self-doubt.

Imposter Syndrome

One of the main reasons for these challenges us the all-too-common experience of imposter syndrome, the nagging feeling that you don't belong or that you're not qualified for the success you've achieved.

The psychological root cause of imposter syndrome typically stems from a combination of personal experiences, cognitive biases, and social factors that create a distorted sense of self-worth. At its core, imposter syndrome often arises from deep-seated self-doubt, where individuals feel they don't deserve their achievements or fear being "found out" as a fraud. Historically, women have been underrepresented in leadership positions, which can create a sense of "otherness" when they do rise to these roles. They may feel as though they don't belong or that they are only occupying these positions because of gender quotas or pure luck, not because of their skills or qualifications.

People with imposter syndrome often set unrealistically high standards for themselves and feel immense pressure to be perfect. When they inevitably fall short, it reinforces the belief that they are inadequate or undeserving. Childhood experiences, particularly in environments with high expectations or overly critical parenting, can shape the way individuals view themselves. If a person grows up feeling they must always achieve to gain approval or avoid criticism, they may carry those feelings of inadequacy into adulthood.

Imposter syndrome is often fuelled by common cognitive distortions, such as catastrophizing, all-or-nothing thinking, and personalization. This is where they believe mistakes or setbacks reflect personal incompetence rather than situational factors. Relying heavily on external validation and recognition can cause a person to doubt their intrinsic worth, making it difficult to internalize successes or see their achievements as truly earned.

Overcoming imposter syndrome starts with a shift in mindset, deep self-awareness, and intentional actions to build confidence. The first and most crucial step is recognizing when you're experiencing it. Naming it, calling it "imposter syndrome", helps you separate fleeting feelings of self-doubt from your actual abilities. Remember, even the most accomplished professionals have struggled with these thoughts. Understanding that imposter syndrome is common, especially among high-achievers, can normalize the experience and remind you that you're not alone.

Once you acknowledge it, the next step is to challenge those negative thoughts. Instead of letting self-doubt dictate your actions, reframe your thinking: Would you speak to a close friend or family member the way you speak to yourself? Probably not. Treat yourself with the same kindness and encouragement you would offer someone else. Keep a record of your accomplishments, big or small. When imposter syndrome creeps in, revisit these wins as proof of your capability and hard-earned success.

Another key strategy is embracing vulnerability. No one is perfect, and growth comes from allowing yourself to make mistakes and learn from them. Rather than fearing failure, view challenges as opportunities to expand your skills. Surround yourself with supportive mentors and colleagues who can offer perspective and remind you of your strengths. Finally, takes actions towards your goals even in times of self-doubt. Confidence is built through experience, not perfection. The more you step out of your comfort zone, the more you'll realize that you are, in fact, worthy of your success.

If self-doubt and panic start creeping in, try asking yourself a series of 'So what?' questions. So, what if you don't have all the answers? So, what if you make a mistake? This simple exercise helps reframe your thinking, reminding you that it's okay to have vulnerabilities and that growth comes from learning along the way.

- o SO, WHAT? You may not yet be the subject matter expert in your field, but that's okay. The fact that you're in the position you are means you already have a solid foundation. Embrace the learning process, nobody starts out knowing everything. Being open about what you don't know not only accelerates your growth but invites others to help you learn faster. Ask more questions, seek feedback, and watch yourself evolve into the expert you want to become. Remember, no one becomes an expert without being curious and unafraid of asking.

- o SO, WHAT? You made a mistake in an email. It happens to everyone! In fact, your colleagues make mistakes too, but you're too busy scrutinizing yourself to notice them. The truth is, people are far less likely to judge you as harshly as you judge yourself. Mistakes are simply stepping stones to improvement, each one teaches you something valuable. Next time, let it go, learn from it, and move on.

o SO, WHAT? You don't know the answer to something you've been asked. Guess what? You don't have to know it all. If someone's asking you, it's probably because they don't have the answer either, and that's okay. Taking a moment to find the answer gives you time to reflect, research, and bring a well-thought-out response. It's more important to be resourceful than to have every answer right off the bat.

o SO, WHAT? You feel like a fraud for being in a leadership role, especially when you think your team members might be more skilled than you are. But here's the truth: great leaders don't need to be the best at everything, they create an environment where others can shine. The best managers empower their teams, highlight their strengths, and build a collaborative space for growth. So, if your team members outshine you in some areas, that's a win! It means you're leading a high-performing, talented group, and your success comes from enabling theirs.

Imposter syndrome is often fuelled by distorted thinking. Combat these negative thoughts by actively challenging them. Ask yourself: "What evidence do I have that supports these thoughts? What evidence contradicts them?" Shift your focus from perceived inadequacies to your actual achievements and strengths. Take time to recognize and celebrate your achievements, no matter how small they may seem.

Reflect on how far you've come and how your efforts have contributed to your successes. This helps reinforce your value and capabilities, making it easier to internalize your accomplishments. Writing down your accomplishments, big and small, can serve as a powerful reminder of your value. When feelings of imposter syndrome arise, look back at your journal to remind yourself of all the moments you've succeeded and the progress you've made.

By implementing these strategies, you can gradually break free and begin to trust your abilities. Remember, combating these feelings takes time, but with patience and persistence, you can shift your mindset and embrace your worth with confidence. Shift your mindset from focusing solely on the end goal, or external validation, to valuing the journey. Understand that success isn't just about achieving a title or position, it's about growth, effort, and continuous improvements.

Toxic work environments

You might also be experiencing a toxic work environment, making you feel displaced in the team or role. These environments are characterized by unhealthy workplace dynamics, poor leadership, lack of support, and an overall culture that fosters stress and dissatisfaction. Toxic environments often have a culture of neglecting or undervaluing employees' contributions. A lack of recognition or a failure to provide positive feedback, can make employees feel invisible and unappreciated.

When workers feel like their efforts are ignored or taken for granted, it can lead to a sense of futility. Bad management is a hallmark of toxic work environments. Managers who are either overly controlling, neglectful, inconsiderate or unsupportive create a sense of instability and confusion. Inconsistent or unfair leadership, lack of guidance, and poor communication can leave employees feeling helpless, leading them to internalize their frustrations and blame themselves, all of which exacerbate burnout.

Toxic workplaces often breed negative behaviours like bullying, gossip, or passive-aggressive interactions. When employees are constantly exposed to harassment or interpersonal conflict, it can create an environment where people feel unsafe or unsupported. In many toxic environments, there's a clear disregard for employees' personal time. With expectations of being "always on," employees feel pressure to be available outside working hours, answering emails or attending meetings during their time off.

Navigating a toxic work environment can feel like walking through a maze, with no clear pathway to escape. You might resolve one issue only to be bombarded with new issues the next day. Even if you work on improving your emotional intelligence, it doesn't magically change how others behave towards you. The reality is that no matter how self-aware or calm you become, the actions and attitudes of those around you can still create chaos, making it all the more challenging to maintain your well-being. We explore toxic work scenarios in further detail in chapter: finding ways to minimise your triggers.

Change the role, don't change for the role

This isn't about avoiding growth or shying away from improvement; it's about playing to your strengths and letting go of the pressure to excel in every area. Instead of stressing over what you're not great at, focus on what you're naturally good at, the tasks and projects that come effortlessly to you. Celebrate your wins, big or small, and pour your energy into refining those strengths.

As a starting point, try better understanding of your personality type, take a Myers-Briggs test or similar. The *Myers-Briggs Type Indicator (MBTI)* is a psychological assessment designed to measure individual personality traits and preferences based on theories of personality types. One of the most intriguing contrasts in the Myers-Briggs personality test is the dynamic between introversion and extroversion.

These terms are often misunderstood, with many assuming they equate to being loud versus quiet or confident versus shy. But here's the twist: introversion and extroversion have nothing to do with volume or boldness. Instead, they describe where you draw your energy. Extroverts recharge by engaging with the external world, thriving in social settings and bustling environments. Introverts, on the other hand, find their energy in solitude, reflection, and quieter spaces. It's less about how you act and more about what fuels your inner battery.

Understanding whether you lean toward introversion or extroversion can be a game-changer in figuring out how you thrive in the workplace. Introverts often excel in roles that require deep focus, independent work, and analytical thinking, such as writing, programming, or research-based positions. They may prefer quieter environments where they can work without constant interruptions.

Extroverts, on the other hand, shine in collaborative, fast-paced settings that involve frequent interaction, like sales, event planning, or leadership roles. Knowing your natural tendencies can also guide how you structure your day, whether you're better off tackling solitary tasks first or starting with energizing meetings. By aligning your work environment and responsibilities with your energy preferences, you can maximize productivity, job satisfaction, and overall well-being.

If you're an introvert who thrives behind a screen and is great with technology, you might struggle with client-facing targets as a sales manager tasked with client dinners and outings. On the flip side, if you're an extrovert that recharges in group conversations, being a solitary data analyst in a remote setting might drain you. Sure, you could push yourself to adapt, but ultimately, that would lead to burnout.

Burnout doesn't just come from physical fatigue; it comes from fighting against your natural rhythms. Whether you're an introvert or an extrovert, working in a way that doesn't align with your personality takes a toll on your well-being.

There are countless rewarding careers out there that play to your strengths, why limit yourself to one that leaves you exhausted and unfulfilled? The key is to find a role that suits who you are and how you thrive.

Comparison is the thief of joy

You might find it hard to enjoy or feel settled in your current role if your mind is constantly racing toward the future or caught up in comparisons to others. It's easy to fall into the trap of focusing on what's missing or what's next, all while casting a negative shadow over your present situation. But this mindset can rob you of the chance to appreciate where you are right now and the opportunities it might hold.

It's natural to compare yourself to others, especially colleagues in similar roles or friends working in the same industry. But constantly measuring your progress against theirs can leave you feeling stuck, guilty, or even frustrated about not being "further ahead" in your career. This mindset not only drains your energy but also risks making you resent your current position, overshadowing the value of where you are right now.

Our tendency to compare ourselves to others is deeply ingrained in our biology and psychology, a behaviour shaped by evolution and amplified by modern society. Psychologist Leon Festinger's Social Comparison Theory explains that we naturally evaluate ourselves against others, especially when no clear benchmarks exist.

Sometimes we compare upward, aspiring to emulate someone more successful, though this can fuel envy or inadequacy. Other times, downward comparisons boost our self-esteem by reminding us of our progress.

In today's social media-fuelled world, these comparisons have been turbocharged, exposing us to a constant stream of curated perfection that often sets impossible standards. While this behaviour can motivate growth, it can also trigger stress and anxiety when unchecked. By understanding the roots of social comparison, we can shift from self-criticism to self-awareness, using it as a tool for growth instead of a source of frustration.

One powerful way to break free from the trap of comparison is to shift your focus to the positives in your current situation. Start by making a list of all the great things your role offers right now, whether it's supportive colleagues, new skills you're learning, or simply a steady pay-check. Gratitude has a way of changing perspective, and by actively recognizing your current benefits, you'll see your present in a more empowering light.

If scrolling through social media or LinkedIn is the root cause of you career envy, it's time to take control. Set boundaries around your screen time and curate your feed to avoid content or updates that trigger those feelings of comparison. Whether it's muting certain accounts or taking a step back from constant updates, prioritizing your mental well-being over a highlight reel will help you focus on your own journey, not someone else's.

When thinking about the future, channel your energy into the opportunities ahead rather than fixating on the frustration of not being there yet. This mindset helps every little step along the way feel worthwhile.

7 Finding meaning in your career

"Life is never made unbearable by circumstances, but only by lack of meaning and purpose." – Viktor Frankl

Our history shapes us

Frankl's work, particularly in his book *Man's Search for Meaning*, emphasizes that purpose gives life direction and resilience, even in the face of suffering. He believed that meaning is something we create through our actions, relationships, and how we face challenges, making it the key to a fulfilling life. Finding meaning in our work often begins with understanding where it all started. The origins of a profession can reveal its deeper purpose, connecting the work we do today with the values of past societies. Professions don't just appear out of nowhere, they're shaped by history, culture, and the evolution of humanity.

When we trace the roots of our careers, we uncover how they connect to a broader, centuries-old story that continues to shape the world today. This perspective transforms our daily tasks from mere routines into meaningful contributions. It also highlights the ways historical inequalities, like those based on gender or race, have influenced certain roles, reminding us how far we've come and how much further we have to go.

By understanding this journey, our jobs can become more than just a pay check; they can serve as sources of purpose and progress. As humans, our innate drive to innovate, improve, and leave a lasting legacy has built the very foundation of today's careers.

Corporate roles, often dismissed as dull or uninspiring, are actually the products of thousands of years of ingenuity. These careers represent the intricate systems humanity has developed to solve problems, foster innovation, and create connections on a global scale. Yet, how often do we pause to acknowledge the legacy we've inherited? Modern workplaces, technologies, and tools didn't materialize overnight, they're the result of relentless progress, shaped by the desire to make work more efficient and life better.

Even the most glamorous jobs, like astronauts, wildlife photographers, or film directors, are grounded in years of preparation and hard work. Astronauts endure gruelling simulations and repetitive maintenance tasks in space. Wildlife photographers face weeks in harsh conditions for a single perfect shot. Directors, despite their creative allure, navigate tedious logistical planning and exhaustive editing. These dream roles may sparkle on the surface, but they're built on discipline and an acceptance of the grind, proving that no job is without its mundane side.

So, what about our corporate careers? Beneath their surface lies unexpected significance and impact, showing that these roles, far from being monotonous, are integral to the world's progress. By shifting our perspective, we can see them not just as jobs, but as vital pieces of a greater story.

Lawyers and Solicitors – the guardians of justice

The legal profession traces its origins to the dawn of civilization, when humanity first recognized the need for structured systems to maintain order and resolve disputes. In the absence of laws, conflicts were often settled through violence or primitive practices, which underscored the necessity of governance.

One of the earliest known legal codes, the Code of Hammurabi (circa 1754 BC), emerged in ancient Babylon, providing a comprehensive framework for everything from property disputes to criminal justice. It also created the demand for interpreters and enforcers, setting the stage for the professionalization of law. Similarly, ancient Egypt, Greece, and Rome developed intricate legal systems, with Roman law laying the groundwork for principles like contracts, property rights, and equitable justice that still underpin many of today's legal frameworks.

The legal profession, as we know it, began to take shape during the Middle Ages. As societies grew more complex, the demand for specialists in legal affairs surged. By the 13th century, universities in Europe were offering formal legal training, distinguishing lawyers from other justice officials. Institutions like the Inns of Court in England played a crucial role in fostering a professional approach to law, setting ethical and procedural standards that resonate today. Major historical events have often acted as catalysts for significant legal developments.

For instance, the Magna Carta of 1215 was born out of tensions between King John of England and his barons, laying the foundation for constitutional governance and individual rights. Similarly, the horrors of World War II spurred the creation of the Universal Declaration of Human Rights in 1948, a ground-breaking document that established fundamental freedoms and inspired legal systems worldwide.

Today, the legal profession remains a cornerstone of justice and societal order. Lawyers and judges uphold individual rights, ensure the equitable application of laws, and influence societal change. Intriguingly, the presumption of innocence, "innocent until proven guilty", finds its roots in Roman law, demonstrating how ancient traditions continue to shape contemporary legal practices. These stories remind us that the law evolves alongside humanity, reflecting our struggles, aspirations, and progress toward a more just society.

Accountants – the business translators

The history of accounting is as ancient as civilization itself, stretching back thousands of years, long before the advent of written language. In the cradle of civilization, Mesopotamia, the need to record trades and manage resources spurred the development of early bookkeeping systems. These pioneering accountants used clay tablets to track exchanges involving crops, livestock, and goods, creating the first rudimentary financial records.

This innovation was essential to the growth of these early societies, creating the foundation for the complex financial systems that of the modern world.

The 15th century marked a pivotal advancement, with the advent of double-entry bookkeeping during the Italian Renaissance. Luca Pacioli, a mathematician and close associate of Leonardo da Vinci, introduced this revolutionary system in his 1494 work, *Summa de Arithmetica, Geometria, Proportioni et Proportionalita*. Pacioli's method of recording debits and credits transformed how businesses managed their finances, enabling them to operate with unprecedented precision and clarity.

In today's world, accounting is often called the "language of business," and for good reason. Far more than just number-crunching, it translates raw financial data into meaningful insights that drive critical decisions. Whether it's guiding the launch of a new product, opening a new warehouse, or navigating through an economic downturn, accounting provides the clarity organizations need to not only survive, but to create actual value.

Accounting, is the invisible force stabilising the economy, providing timely insights into a business's health. It is only through these records and insights, that businesses stand a chance of succeeding in a competitive market. On a broader scale, it's the cornerstone of global economic stability, promoting transparency, trust, and accountability.

Administrators and Assistants – the right-hand man

The administrative profession grew from humanity's attempts to bring order to chaos. In ancient civilizations like Egypt, Mesopotamia, and China, administrators, often scribes or clerks, were crucial for maintaining records, organizing resources, and supporting rulers in managing the state. The Roman Empire, spanning three continents, was a testament to administrative prowess. Its vast bureaucracy enabled Rome to efficiently collect taxes, manage armies, and maintain public infrastructure, demonstrating that no empire can flourish without a robust administrative backbone.

The Industrial Revolution brought seismic changes to the field. As factories churned out goods and businesses expanded, the need for efficient organization skyrocketed. Secretaries, clerks, and office managers became indispensable, ensuring operations ran smoothly in an era of rapid growth. The typewriter and telephone, revolutionary technologies at the time, transformed the workplace, enabling administrators to communicate and document with unprecedented speed and accuracy.

During World War II, administrative professionals played a vital role in both the military and civilian sectors, ensuring the seamless coordination of war efforts. From managing complex supply chains and processing critical intelligence to maintaining troop records and facilitating communication, their meticulous work kept operations running smoothly.

Their dedication and precision were crucial to the Allied victory, highlighting the indispensable role of administrative work in times of global crisis.

Interestingly, the word "secretary" derives from the Latin secretarius, meaning "keeper of secrets," reflecting the discretion and trust central to the role. This couldn't be truer in the remarkable story of Elizabeth Smith Friedman, a U.S. cryptanalyst during the World Wars. Initially hired as a secretary, her administrative skills and sharp intellect led her to break complex enemy codes, saving countless lives and shaping the outcome of critical battles. Today, administrators continue to be the maestros of efficiency across every industry, be it corporations, healthcare, education, business, or government.

The IT crowd – the innovators

The evolution of information technology (IT) is a story of ingenuity and transformation, one that has fundamentally reshaped how we live, work, and connect. The journey began in the mid-20th century with monumental innovations like the ENIAC and UNIVAC in the 1940s and 1950s. These room-sized behemoths, hailed as the first electronic general-purpose computers, required a small army of specialized operators and engineers to perform even the simplest calculations. The era marked the birth of the digital age and laid the groundwork for the IT profession as we know it.

By the 1960s and 1970s, computing had become more practical and accessible. With the introduction of smaller, more affordable machines, new roles emerged, such as systems analysts and programmers. These professionals developed software tailored to business needs, fuelling the adoption of technology in industries ranging from banking to manufacturing.

One pivotal moment was during the NASA's Apollo missions, where computer scientists and programmers played a critical role in landing humans on the moon. Margaret Hamilton, a software engineer, famously led the team that developed the onboard flight software, demonstrating the potential of IT to accomplish what was once thought impossible.

The 1980s and 1990s ushered in a technological revolution with the advent of personal computers and the internet. Suddenly, technology wasn't just for governments and corporations, it was in people's homes. Companies like Apple and Microsoft turned computers into household staples, while the World Wide Web connected the globe like never before. The rise of email, online commerce, and digital entertainment created an unprecedented demand for IT professionals. New roles emerged, including network administrators, database specialists, and IT support staff to ensure users could navigate this new digital frontier.

Today, IT professionals are the architects and engineers of the digital world. IT powers everything from online banking platforms to artificial intelligence in robotics.

Their expertise ensures that our digital infrastructure is secure, reliable, and ever-evolving. The profession continues to shape the future, with innovations like quantum computing, blockchain, and machine learning poised to redefine what's possible. The global IT market, projected to reach $13 trillion by 2030, underscores the profession's importance in solving complex challenges and driving progress.

Customer services – the shopping experience

In the late 19th and early 20th centuries, with the rise of industrialization and mass production, businesses started to focus more on customer experience. Companies like Sears, Roebuck and Co. revolutionized the way businesses engaged with their customers. By offering satisfaction guarantees and emphasizing responsive support, Sears not only built trust but also set a standard for customer-centric practices that became a hallmark of modern commerce.

The rise of consumerism intensified the importance of customer experience. In competitive markets, businesses realized that retaining customers required more than just selling a good product, it necessitated creating positive, memorable interactions. This realization marked the birth of dedicated customer service roles, where professionals became the bridge between companies and their clients, fostering loyalty and ensuring brand reputations thrived.

The technological advances further propelled the customer experience. With the invention of the telephone, businesses could offer real-time support, revolutionizing accessibility and responsiveness. The internet era in the 1990s brought about a seismic shift. The rise of e-commerce giants like Amazon introduced digital customer service tools such as email support, live chat, and self-service portals. Jeff Bezos famously credited Amazon's success to its customer-obsessed culture, with innovative practices like one-click shopping and quick refunds transforming the industry.

Today, customer service professionals are more crucial than ever. They're not just problem-solvers; they're brand ambassadors who gather valuable insights into customer preferences, identify emerging trends, and influence product development. Their work drives innovation and ensures companies stay competitive in a fast-paced marketplace. Businesses that excel in providing virtual support and understanding their customers' challenges earn immense goodwill and loyalty. In an era where customer experience is a key differentiator, exceptional service is no longer just a perk, it's a necessity.

Sales and marketing – brand builders

Sales and marketing have their roots in the earliest forms of trade, dating back to civilizations where bartering and persuasion were essential for commerce. Merchants relied on charisma, trust, and personal relationships to strike deals, showcasing their goods in bustling marketplaces.

Even then, the art of capturing attention was crucial, criers would shout out offerings, painted signs adorned market stalls, and vibrant symbols served as some of the first advertisements.

The Industrial Revolution renewed the profession, reshaping the world of commerce forever. As factories churned out goods at unprecedented rates, businesses faced the task of selling on their surplus. Enter the travelling salesman, a figure who became emblematic of this era, bringing products to people's doorsteps and introducing a personal touch. Around the same time, Sears Roebuck transformed retail with its ground-breaking catalogue brochure, a precursor to e-commerce, that allowed families in rural America to access goods previously out of reach.

By the 20th century, sales and marketing had evolved into sophisticated disciplines. Marketing grew into a science, leveraging consumer psychology, market research, and data to craft compelling campaigns. Innovations like segmentation and psychographics enabled businesses to tailor messages to specific demographics, transforming marketing from mass communication into a targeted art form. Major events such as the post-World War II economic boom spurred innovation, giving rise to iconic campaigns like Coca-Cola's global branding strategy and the advent of jingles that cemented products into cultural memory.

Today, sales and marketing extend far beyond promoting products, they solve problems, connect people, and drive progress.

Sales teams educate and guide consumers, while marketing experts delve into the human psyche, uncovering needs and desires to inspire innovation. Stories of transformative campaigns abound, such as Apple's "Think Different," which redefined branding by celebrating creativity and individuality, or the viral power of social media campaigns like ALS's Ice Bucket Challenge, which raised millions for a cause while driving digital engagement.

More than transactions, sales and marketing catalyse innovation, competition, and societal change. They push businesses to deliver better quality, interpret cultural trends, and even predict the future. In this ever-evolving profession, we are reminded that connection, creativity, and understanding are the true currencies of commerce.

A hopeful future

Imagine a future where the office isn't defined by four walls in a concrete building. Work moves with us, whether we're perched in a high-rise, sipping coffee in a bustling café, or exploring a remote corner of the world. This isn't a distant dream; it's a rapidly evolving reality as technology advances, work-life balance takes centre stage, and sustainability becomes a business imperative. In this future, work isn't confined to a desk, it's a fluid, hybrid experience. The workplace of tomorrow is rewriting the rules. Gone are the rigid, cookie-cutter roles of the past.

Instead, agile, forward-thinking positions are emerging to tackle the opportunities and challenges brought by artificial intelligence (AI) and automation. Consider the rise of AI ethicists, professionals dedicated to ensuring technology aligns with human values and safeguarding against bias. Imagine automation analysts, who oversee systems to enhance human productivity rather than replace it. Carbon footprint analysts and sustainability consultants who will lead companies toward greener operations, balancing innovation with environmental stewardship. Meanwhile, data scientists and machine learning experts who will decode green-data, helping organizations make more impactful decisions.

Picture how virtual and augmented realities will transform the way we collaborate. VR designers will work to create immersive digital workplaces where meetings, training, and brainstorming sessions become exciting, multi-sensory adventures. There are already glimpses of this exciting future. Microsoft's "holoportation" technology, which uses mixed reality to project lifelike avatars into meetings, hints at a workplace where geographical boundaries dissolve.

In this visionary landscape, work is no longer just about productivity, it's about purpose. It's about using technology to connect people, nurture creativity, and shape a better world. This is the future of work: ethical, innovative, and deeply human, where progress and sustainability go hand in hand, unlocking potential for individuals, businesses, and the planet alike.

8 Focus on the good

"Be thankful for what you have; you'll end up having more. If you concentrate on what you don't have, you will never, ever have enough."- Oprah Winfrey

Lead with gratitude

Corporate workplaces can present hurdles, but they also hold extraordinary potential to spark growth, empowerment, and transformation. While the daily grind may sometimes feel monotonous, these roles are far more than just a pay check. They're springboards for mastering new skills, achieving significant accolades, and thriving in dynamic teams that work together toward meaningful goals. Along the way, you'll cultivate connections that often blossom into lifelong friendships and invaluable networks.

Even though your dreams may likely lie beyond the workplace, whether it's building your own business, financial freedom, dedicating time to family, retiring early, or pursuing a passion-driven career like coaching or gardening, your current role is a critical stepping stone. By embracing your present, you unlock the opportunity to develop the expertise, resilience, and confidence needed to shape the future you desire.

The key lies in shifting your mindset. When you view your role as a platform for growth rather than a prison cell, everything changes. Believe in your capacity for progress. Trust that challenges can be overcome and that every step in your journey matters. With this empowering perspective, you can turn your current job into a launchpad for a life. The future is yours to create, one intentional step at a time.

Gratitude, is more than a simple act of thankfulness, it is a powerful force for transformation. It's a tool that rewires your brain, fostering resilience, enhancing self-esteem, and cultivating happiness. By focusing on what's right rather than what's wrong, gratitude creates clarity in chaos and brings you into the present moment. It can boost your emotional well-being and help you connect to your purpose. Gratitude is not just about making lists of what you're thankful for, it's about truly feeling blessed, letting those feelings guide your mindset and actions.

Building the gratitude muscle

Transforming your outlook begins with a shift in perspective. Instead of focusing on what's missing, contrast your life with the challenges others might face. Imagine someone who never had the same opportunities you've enjoyed. Step into their shoes for a moment, feel their struggles, their hopes. Suddenly, the things you take for granted come into sharp focus.

Imagine how extraordinary it would be for them to experience what you now consider routine. Now, look back at your younger self, the version of you filled with dreams, curiosity, and wonder. If they could see you now, how amazed would they be? The challenges you've overcome, the skills you've mastered, the things you once thought were impossible but now do effortlessly, it would feel like pure magic to them. They'd be in awe of your strength, your resilience, and just how far you've come.

Even the you from just a few years ago would be stunned. Think back to when speaking up in meetings felt intimidating, when presenting to colleagues made you nervous, or when engaging with senior leaders felt overwhelming. Those moments that once pushed you outside your comfort zone are now second nature. You've not only met the goals you once set, you've surpassed them. And that's proof of your growth, your adaptability, and your ability to take on whatever comes next.

Now, fast forward. Picture your future self, the person who has achieved everything you dream of today. See yourself standing in that success, feeling the pride and joy that come with it. Imagine looking back at the journey that got you there, the lessons learned, the obstacles conquered, the growth that shaped you. Let that vision fuel you, knowing that every step, including this very moment, is part of the story leading to your ultimate success.

At first, shifting to a positive mindset might feel unnatural, like you're trying to convince yourself of something you don't really believe in. But with practice, gratitude and optimism can become second nature. When you focus on the good, you activate your brain's natural ability to generate happiness, motivation, and resilience. Over time, this shift happens effortlessly. It's not just about reaching an end goal, it's about embracing the journey and recognizing the joy in each milestone.

Now, let's apply this mindset to your career. No matter how routine or challenging your workday feels, try looking at it through a different lens. What skills are you developing? What hidden opportunities exist in your day to day? Every moment offers a lesson, and each challenge you face is a stepping stone toward your future success. By practicing gratitude and shifting your perspective, you can find meaning in the process and fuel the motivation to keep moving forward.

There are countless ways to train your mind to see the best in your situation, boosting both your well-being and your sense of hopeful anticipation. Here are some powerful thought patterns to practice:

- ○ **I'm so grateful to have a competitive salary...** Corporate roles often offer competitive salary packages, often complemented by performance bonuses and incentives. These additional rewards can substantially increase your overall earnings, making corporate careers financially rewarding compared to many other job types.

- ○ **I have a clear path to my future goals...** Many corporate jobs provide clear pathways for career growth. With structured promotion trajectories, professional development opportunities, and access to mentorship.

- ○ **My current role allows me to have job security...** Corporations often offer greater job security compared to smaller businesses or freelance roles. Established companies tend to have more stable financial conditions and offer robust employment contracts.

o **I have an array of options in my benefits package...** Corporate jobs typically offer comprehensive benefits, including health insurance, dental and vision coverage, retirement plans, and paid time off. These perks contribute to overall financial and personal well-being.

o **My networking opportunities can support my future goals...** Working in a corporate environment provides numerous opportunities to build a professional network. This can be valuable for career advancement, learning from industry leaders, and this could open doors to new paths or even building your own business.

o **I am able to develop my skills and get qualifications...** Corporate roles often come with training programs and development initiatives that help employees acquire new skills, enhance existing ones, get qualified in new areas and stay updated with industry trends and technologies.

o **I have special access to resources, such as systems and tools...** Working for a corporation typically means access to extensive resources, including advanced technology, research tools, and support staff, which can enhance productivity and job satisfaction.

- o **My structured role guides me to build a beneficial daily routine...** Corporate jobs usually offer a structured work environment with defined roles, responsibilities, and processes. This structure can provide a sense of stability and clarity in your day-to-day tasks.

- o **I'm able to learn from a lot of interesting and inspiring people...**We often overlook how many great friendships we make through work or how many role models we encounter who genuinely embody the traits and values we are working towards.

Romanticize your day

While the benefits of gratitude are well-known, truly feeling it, especially in the daily routine of our jobs, can be a challenge. That's where the magic of romanticizing your journey comes in. Instead of seeing your work as mundane, reframe it as part of an unfolding story. Imagine yourself as the protagonist of your own movie, where every meeting, presentation, and task is a key scene where you are shining and shaping your path to success. Romanticizing your workday as a woman can also mean infusing it with femininity and little moments of joy that make even the most routine tasks feel special.

Start by curating a morning ritual that sets the tone, perhaps a scented candle as you get ready, a carefully chosen outfit that makes you feel confident, or a warm cup of tea in your favourite mug. Bring softness and beauty into your workspace with fresh flowers, a personal notebook, or ambient music that lifts your spirit.

Throughout the day, embrace intentionality, take mindful breaks to stretch, sip a luxurious latte, or reapply your favourite perfume as a small act of self-care. View your tasks not as obligations, but as part of a grander, more elegant journey toward your dreams.

Whether it's the way you write an email, engage in meetings with poise, or celebrate small wins, find ways to bring warmth, charm, and positive energy into everything you do. By weaving beauty into your day, work transforms from a routine to a more enchanting and fulfilling experience.

Maybe this isn't your dream job yet, but what if this chapter is the foundation for something extraordinary? By romanticizing your journey, you transform the ordinary into something remarkable, making even the most routine days feel like meaningful steps toward greatness.

After all, it's not just about where you are right now, it's about the incredible destination you're moving toward. So, embrace the story you're writing.

Create a journaling routine

A powerful way to tailor this practice to your unique experience is through journaling. Take a moment to jot down all the positive takeaways from your current job, the skills you've gained, the relationships you've built, and the opportunities it has provided. Journaling isn't just reflective; it's transformative. Research published in *The Journal of Experimental Psychology* shows that journaling significantly boosts cognitive processing and happiness. Participants who practiced daily gratitude journaling reported noticeable improvements in well-being and overall satisfaction.

If sticking to a regular journaling routine feels daunting at first, start small. Begin with a one-time list of everything you appreciate about your current role. Over time, you can build on this foundation, making journaling a rewarding habit that enhances your mental and emotional well-being. To make it even more engaging, incorporate visualizations into your journaling. Use Pinterest to create mood boards or find images online that represent the goals and experiences you're aiming for. Pairing these visuals with your reflections elevates the practice, turning it into a creative and inspiring ritual that keeps you motivated and aligned with the life you're striving to create.

Journaling can be as simple as grabbing a notebook and pen or as digital as using apps like Day One, Evernote, or OneNote. Even basic note-taking apps can help you capture your thoughts digitally, making it easy to journal on the go.

If writing isn't your thing, try recording your thoughts, speaking can be just as effective for capturing reflections and emotions. Experiment with different methods to find what feels most natural for you.

The hardest part is often getting started, writing or recording that first word can feel like a huge hurdle. But there are several ways to break through this initial barrier and kick-start your journaling habit:

- o Free Writing: Set a timer for 10-15 minutes and write whatever comes to mind without worrying about grammar or structure.

- o Prompts: Use journaling prompts to spark ideas. Prompts can be questions like, "What am I grateful for today?" or "What challenges did I face this week?"

- o Stream of Consciousness: Write continuously without censoring yourself, which can help uncover deeper thoughts and feelings.

- o Reflective Journaling: Reflect on specific events or experiences, analysing your reactions and emotions.

- o Mind Mapping: Create visual diagrams to explore ideas or solve problems.

Finding the ideal time to journal can transform your writing practice into a powerful daily ritual. If you're a morning person, journaling can be a refreshing way to set a positive tone for the day, clearing your mind and sparking creativity before the world wakes up. For those who prefer a midday pause, a quick journaling session can help you realign with your goals and recharge your focus.

In the evening, reflecting on the day's events and processing your thoughts can offer a sense of closure and help you unwind. And if you're looking to end the day on a serene note, journaling before bed can clear your mind of lingering worries, promote gratitude, and pave the way for a restful night's sleep. Ultimately, the best time to journal is whenever you can carve out a moment of calm and connection with yourself, so experiment with different times to find what suits you best.

In order to tailor your journaling to help you in experiencing more gratitude towards your current job and the career path you've had, consider using some of the following prompt:

- "What positive experience did I encounter at work today?" – A simple way to focus on positive aspects.

- "What are my top three priorities today?" – Helps you set clear goals and stay focused.

o "Describe a recent challenge and how I overcame it." – Encourages problem-solving and reflection on personal growth.

o "What is something I'll be doing this week that will help to elevate me to my next position?" – Shifts focus to positive expectations and anticipation.

o "What did I learn on the job today and how can I apply it in future?" – Promotes self-improvement and recognition of daily lessons.

o "How did I positive influence and support others at work today?" – Encourages emotional awareness and understanding.

o "What did I do today that I'm proud of?" – Builds confidence and acknowledges achievements.

o "If I could offer advice to my younger self, what would it be?" – Facilitates self-reflection and insight.

o "What is something I'd like to improve about myself?" – Helps in identifying areas for personal development.

o "Describe a little or a big win that I achieved today." – Connects with your achievements and helps prepare you for your appraisals.

o "What is one little luxury I enjoyed during my working day?" – You might have had an amazing coffee at the coffee shop near your office, or you might have indulged in a lunchtime browse at your favourite shop and bought something you love. Romanticise every little thing and you'll watch your life bloom.

Hack your psychology towards gratitude

Of course, it is easier said than done. We might all be able to understand these concepts and at a surface level, we often struggle to emotionally feel this gratitude within ourselves. It is this feeling, coupled with the positive thoughts, that can bring that profound sense of ease and wellbeing in our daily lives in spite of any adversities. Sometimes, we need to hack our own psychology and body chemistry, to bring about these feelings and ensure they remain our baseline in the long run.

Sound frequencies can be a game-changer when it comes to boosting your mood and keeping your thoughts positive. The science behind how music frequencies affect the body is rooted in how sound interacts with our brain and nervous system. Sound waves are essentially vibrations that travel through air, water, and even solid objects, so when we listen to music, these vibrations enter the body and interact with our cells and tissues.

Binaural beats, for example, play two slightly different frequencies in each ear, creating a calming effect that can reduce anxiety and promote relaxation. Isochronic tones, with their pulsing rhythms, help you get into a relaxed or focused state, perfect for enhancing your meditation practice and lifting your mood. Even nature sounds, like birds chirping or ocean waves, have been shown to ease stress and elevate mood. Plus, listening to upbeat music or meditative tunes can create a positive atmosphere and help shift your focus away from negativity.

Ancient Solfeggio frequencies, like the soothing 528 Hz, are believed to promote healing and love, adding a touch of positivity to your day. Ancient Solfeggio frequencies are like hidden keys in music, believed to unlock parts of the mind, body, and spirit. Imagine tones that do more than sound good, they might actually soothe, heal, and transform. Rooted in the sacred chants of monks and mystics, these frequencies have been used for centuries to foster peace and connection, with each tone resonating on a unique wavelength that taps into different energies.

A fascinating study out of Japan explored the potential of 528 Hz, the so-called "miracle" frequency, to reduce stress and boost well-being. Researchers played 528 Hz music for participants and closely monitored stress biomarkers. The results, published in the Journal of Addiction Research & Therapy, were striking: not only did stress levels drop, but cortisol a hormone tied to stress, showed significant reductions.

Participants also reported feeling more energized and uplifted after listening. The study didn't just stop at people; animals exposed to the same frequency experienced a decrease in oxidative stress, suggesting that 528 Hz could have a protective, anti-stress effect on cells themselves.

Here's a glimpse into what each one does:

- 396 Hz is called the "Liberation Frequency," and it's all about releasing heavy feelings like guilt, fear, or anxiety, allowing you to step into freedom.

- 417 Hz is known as the "Undoing Frequency" and is thought to help you let go of past pain, clearing the way for change and new beginnings.

- 528 Hz, or the "Miracle Tone," is perhaps the most magical of all, said to inspire transformation and even encourage cellular repair at a fundamental level.

- 639 Hz goes by the "Connection Frequency," and it's like a bridge-builder, thought to nurture harmony in relationships and deepen empathy.

- 741 Hz, the "Awakening Frequency," is associated with mental clarity, said to sharpen intuition and help the body release toxins.

o 852 Hz, called the "Spiritual Order Frequency," rounds out the set, enhancing spiritual awareness and that deep sense of connectedness.

Today, these frequencies have surged in popularity, appearing in meditation music, wellness apps, and healing practices. Though science is still catching up on how they might work, many listeners describe feeling more grounded, relaxed, or even uplifted. Whether it's ancient mysticism or a real sonic balm, Solfeggio frequencies are a fascinating invitation to explore a deeper, resonant harmony within.

By tapping into these sound frequencies, you can create a mental environment that fosters calm and positivity, whilst practising gratitude towards all of the positive aspects you can think of or journal. Using one of the many music apps available, like Spotify or Amazon Music, search for these playlists to curate your mood boosting soundscape. Keep them handy, create a folder, and get these playing anytime you feel a disconnect between the thoughts you are working through and the feelings of gratitude you are trying to invoke.

If you need a further sensory boost that sharpens your focus and clears your mind to help you journal better, scents can provide just that. Scents and smells, like sound frequencies, have a profound impact on our minds and bodies, triggering powerful emotional and physical responses.

When we inhale a scent, molecules travel through the nose to the olfactory bulb, directly connecting to the limbic system, the part of the brain responsible for memory, emotion, and behaviour. This is why certain scents, such as lavender or chamomile, can immediately soothe and calm us, helping to reduce anxiety and promote relaxation.

Scents also influence our physical state, as studies have shown lavender and sandalwood can lower blood pressure and heart rate, inducing a "rest and digest" response that counters stress. Others, like citrus or peppermint, can increase alertness, boost energy, and improve focus. Peppermint, with its invigorating zest, wakes up your senses and sharpens your alertness, while the fresh, tangy aroma of lemon can brighten your mood and help you zero in on your tasks. Eucalyptus offers a crisp, refreshing breeze that clears mental fog, making way for clarity. Rosemary's herbaceous scent enhances memory and concentration, perfect for when you need to stay sharp.

Aromatherapy, a practice using essential oils, taps into this powerful mind-body connection, helping to relieve pain, improve mood, and even support immune function. Whether through scent or sound, these natural stimuli interact with the nervous system in ways that uplift, calm, and restore us, making our senses invaluable tools for wellness. Embrace these scents through essential oils, candles, or diffusers, and transform your day into a haven of clarity.

9 Assess your core values

"Your core values are the deeply held beliefs that authentically describe your soul." –
John C. Maxwell

Focus and clarity

If you lack clarity on your core values, you forfeit your connection to your true self. To truly thrive in your work and life, you need a clear sense of purpose, something that aligns deeply with what matters most to you. Identifying your core values isn't just a self-discovery exercise; it's the foundation upon which your future goals are built, shaping every decision you make. Your values are the compass that guide you through personal and professional choices, ensuring you stay focused on what truly fulfils you.

When you are in tune with your core values, your goals evolve from mere tasks into purposeful steps. They become milestones on a journey of growth, resilience, and authentic success, reflecting what truly matters to you and what gives your life depth. By regularly reflecting on these values, you create a life where your actions resonate with your beliefs and passions, ensuring that each effort you make leads to a greater sense of fulfilment, clarity, and lasting satisfaction.

Author Bronnie Ware, who published the book: *The Top Five Regrets of the Dying,* spent many years working with end of life patients in palliative care. Her patients opened up with their life stories, reflecting on their past and divulging how they wish they could have lived. The number one regret that these individuals experienced was the regret of not living authentically to themselves.

A powerful quote from the book captures this realisation beautifully; "I wish I'd had the courage to live a life true to myself, not the life others expected of me". Many people lamented not having the courage to live authentically, chasing their own dreams rather than conforming to societal expectations. They wish they had prioritized relationships over material pursuits, recognizing that true joy comes from nurturing connections with loved ones.

The suppression of their feelings emerged as a common lament; they craved the freedom to express their emotions and have heartfelt conversations that could have enriched their lives. Many came to understand that they stifled their own happiness, letting the grind of daily routines eclipse the joy that should be at the forefront of their lives. Bronnie Ware's insights serve as a powerful rallying cry, urging us to live boldly, cherish our relationships, express our true selves and embrace change. In doing so, we can craft lives filled with meaning and free from the burdens of regret.

The first step in the right direction to live authentically, is to know what it is that you most value and what it is you want to pursue. When it comes to making decisions, your core values act as a foundational framework.

This alignment makes your decisions more authentic and confident, as you're not just reacting to circumstances but acting according to what you believe is right. Moreover, understanding your core values can significantly boost your motivation. When your goals are in sync with what you value most, you're naturally more passionate and driven, making it easier to persist through challenges.

Core values also play a crucial role in building authentic relationships. They shape how you interact with others and what you seek in connections. By being clear about your values, you can forge stronger, more genuine relationships with people who share similar beliefs, leading to more meaningful and supportive connections. When your actions align with your values, you build trust both with yourself and with others, creating a strong sense of personal integrity and respect. Ultimately, core values provide a sense of direction and meaning in life. When your goals and actions align with your values, you create a life that feels purposeful and rewarding.

Identify core values

So, what are examples of core values that can reflect both in the workplace and in aspects of our personal lives?

Achievement	Balance	Connection	Enjoyment
Adventure	Belonging	Consistency	Equality
Ambition	Calmness	Creativity	Frugality
Leadership	Confidence	Decisiveness	Generosity
Appreciation	Commitment	Determination	Harmony
Authenticity	Compassion	Empathy	Patience
Kindness	Loyalty	Service	Passion

Sometimes differing values can contradict each other, so it's important to be super clear which you prioritise.

In the workplace

The corporate environment can be challenging, with frequent pressures and ethical dilemmas. Having a strong understanding of your core values provides a stable foundation that helps you navigate these challenges with confidence. Understanding your core values helps you make career choices that align with your principles. Whether it's choosing the right company to work for, deciding on a career path, or evaluating job offers, knowing what matters most to you ensures that your decisions support your long-term success and a deeper sense of satisfaction.

For instance, if fairness and justice is at the heart of your core values, then you'll naturally be drawn to organizations that prioritize more ethical practices. If teamwork is your priority, then working in a collaborative environment will likely bring you more satisfaction than a job where you work in isolation. For leaders, values are even more essential. They are the bedrock of authentic and impactful leadership. Leading with integrity not only earns the trust and respect of your team but also sets the tone for a positive and cohesive workplace culture. A leader who values respect, for example, will foster an environment where every voice is heard and every contribution appreciated.

Applying it in practice

To pinpoint your core values, begin by reflecting on the experiences that have brought you the deepest sense of fulfilment. What moments made you feel truly alive, proud, or at peace? Consider the principles at play during these times, were they centred on growth, connection, integrity, or creativity? Take note of the qualities you admire in others, as these often mirror what you value most in yourself. Likewise, pay attention to situations that triggered a strong emotional response, whether positive or negative, as these reactions can reveal what truly matters to you. Assessing your core values in practice involves a thoughtful, reflective process.

Here's a step-by-step approach with real-life examples to help you identify and clarify your core values:

- ○ **Reflect on Key Life Experiences**
  Think about the moments in your life when you've felt truly fulfilled or proud. Maybe it was leading a project at work that exceeded expectations, or perhaps it was the sense of joy you felt while volunteering for a cause close to your heart. These experiences were more than just accomplishments, they were moments where your core values came to life. Now, take a moment to reflect. Why did those experiences feel so meaningful to you? What values were driving those emotions?

- ○ **Identify Inspirational Figures**
  Consider people you admire, whether they are public figures, mentors, or personal acquaintances. What qualities or values do they embody that you find inspiring?
  Maybe it's a community leader whose compassion and commitment to social justice resonates with you, or a colleague whose innovation drives positive change. These traits often reflect what's most important to you, thus driving your admiration.
  Write down a list of your role models and the values you associate with them. Once you have your list, take a moment to reflect on how these values connect with your own beliefs and how they shape the choices you make in life.

o **Assess Your Emotional Responses**

Reflect on situations where you felt a strong emotional response, either positive or negative. Perhaps, you felt particularly upset during a situation where you perceived unfairness or dishonesty from someone you trust. It might indicate that fairness and honesty are core values for you.

Pay attention to how your reactions reveal what you truly care about and what principles you hold close. These emotional responses can guide you in understanding what matters most to you.

o **Consider Your Passions and Interests**

Reflect on the activities or causes that ignite your passion. Whether it's a creative outlet, a sport, mentoring others or volunteering, these pursuits often point to deeper values like service to others or collaboration.

Curate and maintain a list of hobbies, volunteer activities, and causes you are drawn to try or have enjoyed in the past. Ask yourself what values they reveal and how they connect to your larger goals. Fill your schedule with activities that not only bring personal joy and entertain you, but that also serve your greater purpose.

Create the identity that you want for yourself

Once you've identified your core values, take a moment to craft a personal statement that encapsulates these guiding principles. For example, you might write: "I value creativity, connection, and balance. I am committed to brining innovative solutions to projects at my work, while ensuring my personal life is enriched with joy and well-being." This clear and concise statement can serve as your compass, helping you make decisions and set goals that are aligned with what matters most to you.

When setting professional goals, make sure they are in harmony with your core values. For example, if work-life balance is one of your top priorities, establish goals that support both your career aspirations and personal well-being. This might include seeking flexible work arrangements, carving out time for family and self-care, or ensuring that your work schedule allows for rest and relaxation.

How to approach conflicting values

Core values can conflict with each other when you hold multiple values that, in certain situations, pull you in different directions or demand different actions. This can happen in various aspects of life, including personal decisions, relationships, and professional settings.

Here are a few examples of how these conflicts can arise:

Values	Challenges
Work-Life Balance	One common conflict occurs between values related to career ambition and family or personal time. For example, if you highly value both professional success and spending quality time with your family, you might face a dilemma when a demanding job opportunity arises. Pursuing the career opportunity may require long hours and significant travel, which could limit the time you spend with your loved ones, causing tension between these two important values.
Honesty vs. Compassion	Another example is the conflict between honesty and compassion. If you value honesty, you might feel compelled to give blunt, but constructive, feedback in a situation where someone's feelings could be triggered. On the other hand, if you also value compassion, you may struggle with how to deliver that feedback in a way that is kind and considerate. Balancing the need to be critically truthful with the desire to be empathetic can create internal conflict.

Independence vs. Collaboration	Values of independence and collaboration can also clash. If you strongly value independence, you may prefer to work alone and make decisions on your own. However, if you also value collaboration, you might find it challenging to navigate situations where teamwork and collective decision-making are required. Balancing these values can be difficult, especially when both are necessary for success.
Security vs. Adventure	Some people value both security (stability, safety) and adventure. A conflict might arise when an exciting but risky opportunity presents itself, such as moving to a new city or starting your own business. Choosing the adventurous path might threaten your sense of security, while sticking with the safe option could feel like missing out on an exciting new chapter.
Tradition vs. Innovation	You might also experience a conflict between valuing tradition (upholding long-standing customs or beliefs) and valuing innovation (embracing change and new ideas). For instance, in a long-established brand or business, you may value the traditional ways of running the business but also recognize the need for innovative approaches to stay competitive. Deciding whether to stick with tradition or push for innovation can create tension.

Sometimes it is necessary, in order to get clarity when dealing with situations that put any of your core values in conflict, to tap into your gut feeling. Not everything is solved by endless analysis and logic. We often know deep down what the right decision is, when we quiet the noise of our minds. Consider the context of the situation and ask yourself questions like:

- o Is this conflict short-term or long-term?
- o How significant is this decision in the broader scope of my life or career?
- o Are there external factors, such as timing or the needs of others, that influence which value should take precedence?

Reflect on your priorities, think about which value aligns more closely with your current self and your long-term vision. In some situations, certain values may be more relevant or critical than others. Reflect on what matters most to you in this particular phase of your life. Evaluate the potential outcomes of prioritizing one value over the other. What are the possible positive and negative consequences? How will your decision impact your life, relationships, and well-being?

Putting this into practice

Picture this: you're faced with a tough decision where your love for adventure is clashing with your need for stability.

You've been offered an incredible job opportunity abroad, one that's hard to pass up. But then there's the life at home that you've meticulously built, the relationships you've nurtured, and the financial security you've worked so hard for. So, applying the reflection points discussed above, you might assess this decision by:

- **Is this conflict short-term or long-term?** In this case, it might be long-term. If you leave your current job and start a new one abroad, you would wisely want to ensure you spend sufficient time at the new job to gain the right experience, skills and boost your CV as a result.

- **How significant is this decision in the broader scope of my life or career?** This can depend. If the new role is a significant jump and provides a leap on the career ladder, then it might outweigh any impacts to your current life. If it is not a significant change, then you might have concerns over leaving behind family and friends for a role that does not catapult your career growth.

- **Are there external factors, such as timing or the needs of others, that influence which value should take precedence?** Needs of others could include partners, children or family members. If you were going through a hard time, with a family member in ill health, then you might value the quality time and connection with them over the big move.

Moving abroad might seem thrilling, but with all these factors in play, it could feel like a daunting decision. It's not always easy, but knowing your core values can really help you make these decisions more quickly and with greater confidence, giving you peace of mind once you've made the call.

Lean into the decision

Once you've concluded on a big decision, commit to it. Even if doubts linger, accept the decision wholeheartedly. Major life choices rarely come with absolute certainty, and that's completely normal. Embrace the uncertainty as part of the journey. Indecisiveness is an interplay of cognitive overload and fear. When faced with an abundance of choices, our brains can become overwhelmed, leading to what psychologists call "analysis paralysis," where the sheer volume of information stifles clear thinking and prevents action. Emotionally, the fear of making the wrong decision can trigger anxiety, as the amygdala, the brain's emotional centre, becomes hyperactive.

Embracing a decision means actively sticking to it and cultivating the discipline to see it through. This involves not just thinking about it, but also implementing strategies and practices that reinforce your commitment, transforming your intent into action.

Imagine you've taken the bold step to move abroad and start a new career, but suddenly, the fear begins to creep in. The excitement of the opportunity quickly gets overshadowed by doubt. Instead of letting fear takeover, it's time to start romanticizing your new adventure! Dive into the excitement by creating a Pinterest board filled with inspiration for your future home, pictures of the new city, the country's culture, and all the fun adventures that await.

Join online communities of fellow expats who've successfully made the leap and share their experiences, or start building connections with colleagues at your new job. Immerse yourself in the local culture, customs, and etiquette to not only enriche your experience but also to help you navigate social situations with confidence and ease. By immersing yourself in this journey even before you arrive, you'll shift your mindset, transforming that anxiety into pure anticipation.

10 Design your daily routine

"Happiness is not something you postpone for the future, it is something you design for the present" – Jim Rohn

Joyful habits

Designing your dream day is truly life-changing because it empowers you to create a daily routine that aligns with your goals. By imagining your ideal day, you're setting a clear intention for how you want to invest your time and energy, making every moment count. When you design your dream daily routine, you're essentially mapping out a blueprint for living your life with purpose. Whether it's setting aside time for deep work, exercise, self-care, or personal development, having a structured schedule ensures that your priorities don't get lost in the chaos of daily life.

By setting intentional habits and structuring your day, you eliminate the guesswork and reduce decision fatigue, allowing you to channel your energy into what truly matters. A well-planned routine helps build consistency, turning small, productive actions into long-term success. More importantly, routines create a sense of stability, reducing stress and increasing confidence in your ability to manage responsibilities.

When you take charge of your time, you gain clarity and momentum, making it easier to reach your goals and feel empowered in the process. Studies have consistently shown that individuals who are organized and plan out their daily routines tend to outperform their peers in the workplace. Structured routines help reduce procrastination, improve time management, and enhance focus, allowing employees to complete tasks more efficiently and with greater accuracy.

Research also suggests that organized individuals experience lower stress levels, as they are better equipped to manage workloads and meet deadlines without feeling overwhelmed. Additionally, having a clear plan for the day frees up mental energy for creative problem-solving and strategic thinking. Employers often recognize these traits as indicators of reliability and leadership potential, leading to greater career growth and success.

The Magic of manifesting

At the core of manifesting is the idea that our recurring thoughts and feelings can influence our reality. Every thought carries energy, and that energy shapes the world we perceive around us. Think of it like tuning a radio station. If you're constantly tuned to negativity, self-doubt, or fear, that's the signal you'll pick up. But when you focus on positivity, opportunity, and abundance, you start to see more or that and attract more of that into your life.

It starts with clarity and visualization. You have to get crystal clear about what you want, be it success, relationships, or personal growth. Visualization is like mentally rehearsing your desired outcome, imagining yourself already living in that reality. It's about painting the picture so vividly in your mind that it feels real.

But here's the catch: manifesting isn't just about sitting back and thinking positive thoughts. You also need to take aligned action. Picture this: you want a new job. Visualizing yourself in that dream role is a great start, but it won't get you hired unless you take steps toward it—whether that's applying for jobs, updating your resume, or building your network. Manifesting is a dance between intention and action. It's not about waiting for the universe to hand you what you want on a silver platter, but meeting it halfway with purpose-driven moves.

Take baby steps

Although so many of us would be quick to say our dream days would be spent on a tropical beach, if we suddenly woke up and lived this reality there would quickly be many things from your current life you would miss. Not everyone that escapes to a tropical destination does so because they won big in the lottery. Often that tropical beach life might be accompanied by a job in the hotel and leisure industry, working with hundreds of tourists a week and working over weekends.

For some, this would be a dream come true, spending every day immersed in tropical tourism. But for others, it could easily turn into something repetitive or even a distraction from their true passions and goals.

In this scenario, the friends and family you once had living nearby would now be so far away, and suddenly, the comfort of home might become something you crave again. This is why it's important to be mindful of what you already have. Often, the life you're living now might already be a stepping stone in the right direction toward your dream life. Instead of always waiting for the future in order to be happy, learn to appreciate the present while still striving toward your goals. Your current job could be laying the groundwork for the dream life you're building.

If you already have super clear goals, values and you've explored your hobbies in depth, then you might truly know exactly what you want. In which case the decision, like making a big move to the other side of the world for example, will come a lot easier than it does for others. On the other hand, if you aren't quite yet sure what the big picture goal is, focus on the smaller steps.

The cognitive power of planning

The science behind planning your daily schedule is rooted in how the brain functions best with structure, routine, and clear goals. It's not just about organization, it's about unlocking cognitive power and managing mental energy.

Every day, our brains are bombarded with decisions, and without a plan, it's easy to feel overwhelmed. This is where the concept of decision fatigue comes into play. Our brains have a limited capacity for making decisions each day. By planning ahead, you reduce the need for constant decision-making, conserving mental energy for the tasks that truly matter.

A well-planned day also taps into the brain's reward system. Every time you check something off your to-do list, your brain releases dopamine, the "feel-good" neurotransmitter responsible for motivation and pleasure. This simple act of crossing off a task creates a positive feedback loop, encouraging you to keep going. The more you achieve, the more motivated you feel, a cycle that fuels productivity. But beyond productivity, there's a sense of psychological relief that comes with knowing exactly what needs to be done next. It reduces stress and anxiety, creating a sense of control over your day.

Finally, consistent planning helps to build long-lasting habits. The more you plan, the easier it becomes. Over time, your brain starts to automate certain behaviours, turning daily planning into a habit that requires less effort. This is thanks to the basal ganglia, the part of the brain responsible for habit formation. Through repetition, you strengthen neural pathways, making these actions almost automatic. When your brain becomes accustomed to a routine, productivity becomes second nature, and success is no longer a distant goal, but a result of your daily discipline.

Start the morning right

It's about creating a routine that energizes you, sets a positive tone for the day, and aligns with your goals. The perfect morning is a deliberate mix of habits and rituals that reflect who you are and what you need to thrive.

Consider your energy levels and needs when planning out your first few actions of the day:

- o **Physical well-being:** Do you want to focus on fitness or mindful movement? Perhaps if you have an earlier start than others, an intense workout in the morning might not be right for you, but a brisk walk or some morning yoga might.

- o **Mental clarity:** Are you seeking a calm, reflective start with meditation or journaling? If you are waking up with racing thoughts and a clouded mind, these habits might help clear the path for a calm and focused morning.

- o **Productivity:** Do you want to get a head start on work or personal projects? This depends on how your energy levels flow during the day, you might be super focused in the morning and want to focus on harder, more detailed tasks. Alternatively, you might feel your creative juices flowing first thing and want to do your big thinking tasks first.

A successful morning often begins the night before. Plan your next day by writing down priorities, setting out your clothes, or prepping meals. A solid night's sleep is critical, so establish a bedtime routine that ensures you wake up feeling refreshed. This could include winding down with a book, limiting screen time, or enjoying a cup of tea.

How you wake up sets the tone for the rest of the day. Whether you're an early bird or prefer a slower start, find a wake-up strategy that works for you. It could be using a gentle alarm, natural light, or even a wake-up playlist. Stretching or deep breathing right as you wake up can help shake off grogginess and energize your body.

Recommended read: The Power of your senses – Russell Jones

In this book there is an excellent section on how to set the tone for a refreshing sleep and the importance of waking up gently in the mornings. The author refers to a particular alarm sound he created and made available on Spotify called 'Rose Garden Alarm' which is part of this senses book. This alarm is designed to gently wake listeners using a 20-minute crescendo of natural bird songs. Its goal is to align with your circadian rhythm, creating a calming and natural wake-up experience.

Example of a Relaxing Morning Routine

o 7:30 AM – Wake up with a gentle alarm or natural light
o 7:40 AM – Walk, stretch or practice light yoga to awaken the body
o 8:00 AM – Meditate or journal for 10-20 minutes to centre the mind
o 8:30 AM – Enjoy a nutritious breakfast to fuel your brain for the day
o 8:45 AM – Review your goals or to-do list for the day
o 9:00 AM – Dive into a focused work session or personal projects

Plan your perfect day

Once you've mastered your morning routine and gained mental clarity about your goals, it's time to think bigger. Imagine how you would truly live if money weren't a concern, not in terms of the things you'd buy or the luxury of never working again, but how you'd actually spend your days. Regardless of wealth, everyone needs a purpose, a passion, or a project. Even with unlimited resources, you'd still feel a pull toward certain activities, causes, and places that resonate with you.

True abundance is only meaningful when it's paired with mental well-being. Your ideal routine should nurture not just your productivity, but your inner peace. If you had all the money in the world, would you stop taking care of yourself?

Would you give up exercising or engaging in activities that strengthen your mind and body? Hopefully not, because without maintaining your health, nothing else would matter. Wealth is only truly enjoyable when you're in the right mental and physical state to embrace it.

Start with your priorities, look back at your key values and assess the activities that align with this. Consider breaking these down into three categories:

- **Work/Business:** how do you want to work each day? Do you prefer daily team meetings to keep projects on track or more irregular catch-ups? Do you want to take calls in the afternoon to leave your mornings for focus? Do you want to hold time for 30 minutes of daily learning or upskilling your career each day?

- **Personal Goals:** Exercise, hobbies, or self-improvement. What workouts do you enjoy and want to stay dedicated to? What hobbies do you want to find time for each day?

- **Self-Care:** Rest, mindfulness, or mental health breaks. Consider how you want to relax; do you want intermittent breaks all day or do you want to focus on longer periods of work so that you can switch off earlier in the day completely.

Time blocking

Time blocking is like crafting a masterpiece of your day, transforming chaos into a symphony of productivity. Begin with the morning's golden hours, setting a positive tone through invigorating activities like exercise, a nourishing breakfast, and personal growth. As your energy peaks, reserve these precious hours for deep work and creative endeavours. But don't forget the art of balance, schedule regular short breaks to refresh your mind and keep distractions at bay.

In the afternoon, shift gears to handle lighter tasks like emails, administrative duties, or meetings. As the sun sets, transition into your evening block, carving out space for relaxation, family time, or winding down. By orchestrating your day with these time blocks, you create a structured rhythm that maximizes productivity and well-being.

11 Practising self-awareness

"Meditation is the discovery that the point of life is always arrived at in the immediate moment." – Alan Watts

The power of presence

At its core, meditation is a practice of focused attention and self-awareness that encourages deep reflection and inner stillness. It is about quieting the mind, letting go of distractions, and cultivating a sense of presence in the moment. Through techniques like breath control, mantra repetition, visualization, or observing one's thoughts without judgment, meditation allows individuals to deepen their connection with themselves and the world around them. The practice fosters mindfulness, a state of heightened awareness and clarity that can lead to greater emotional balance, peace, and insight.

In many spiritual traditions, meditation is the path to enlightenment, described as a profound realization of one's true nature and the interconnectedness of all things. Enlightenment, or nirvana in Buddhism, is often described as a state of ultimate peace, freedom from suffering, and liberation. It's not just an intellectual understanding but a direct experience, an awakening to the present moment and the impermanence of all things.

114

Spiritual teachings emphasize that enlightenment is marked by an absence of ego and attachment, a sense of boundless compassion, and an overwhelming clarity of mind.

Meditation's history is a fascinating journey that spans thousands of years, woven into the fabric of numerous religious and philosophical traditions around the world. In ancient history, meditation became a cornerstone of spiritual practice, with the ancient Vedas mentioning "Dhyana," a deep meditative state aimed at connecting the mind with higher realms. As meditation spread, it found a profound expression in Buddhism through the teachings of Siddhartha Gautama, the Buddha. His meditative practices, designed to bring about mindfulness and liberation from suffering, spread across Asia, influencing a wide array of traditions.

The modern era saw meditation's journey cross into the West, where it was embraced and explored by spiritual seekers and eventually the scientific community. Figures like Swami Vivekananda and Maharishi Mahesh Yogi were pivotal in introducing Eastern meditation to Western audiences, where it flourished. Today, meditation is not only a spiritual practice but a scientifically-backed tool for enhancing mental and emotional well-being, integrated into everything from mindfulness-based therapies to corporate wellness programs. It's a practice that has transcended its ancient roots to become a global phenomenon, accessible to all who seek inner peace and clarity. Meditation, is backed by a robust body of scientific research that reveals its profound effects on the brain and body.

The science behind it

Scientifically, meditation reshapes the brain itself, a phenomenon known as neuroplasticity. Regular practice strengthens the prefrontal cortex, enhancing decision-making, focus, and self-control, while also regulating the amygdala, reducing stress and emotional reactivity. For those who struggle with stress, meditation's impact on in amygdala activity translates to a calmer, more composed outlook on life.

An analysis published in *Psychological Bulletin* showed that mindfulness meditation resulted in a significant improvement in emotional well-being, with participants reporting a 20% increase in positive emotions and a 10% decrease in negative ones. But the benefits of meditation extend far beyond stress relief. People who meditate regularly experience increased grey matter in the hippocampus, a region associated with memory.

Research conducted by Harvard University (Luders, E., et al. 2015) found that eight weeks of mindfulness meditation led to an increase in grey matter density. This structural change underpins the cognitive and emotional benefits many meditators report. The impact of meditation on attention and focus is equally remarkable. The practice has even been shown to influence brainwave activity, increasing alpha waves associated with relaxation and theta waves linked to deep meditation and creativity, further contributing to a state of calm and clarity.

This suggests that those who meditate consistently are not just calming their minds; they're actually enhancing their cognitive functions. Beyond its mental benefits, meditation also offers profound physical advantages. It strengthens the immune system and aids in pain management by altering the brain's perception of discomfort. Additionally, meditation may play a role in slowing cognitive decline, as research suggests it can influence the length of telomeres, the protective caps on our DNA that shorten with age. These findings highlight meditation's potential to enhance overall health and even contribute to longevity.

In today's fast-paced world, where stress and anxiety are rampant, meditation offers a scientifically proven method to cultivate inner peace, sharpen the mind, and improve overall well-being. Whether you're looking to reduce stress, enhance focus, or boost your health, the science of meditation provides compelling evidence that this ancient practice is a valuable addition to modern life.

Benefits in the workplace

Meditation brings a wealth of benefits to the workplace, transforming not just individual well-being but also enhancing the overall workplace environment. One of the most immediate and noticeable effects is stress reduction. By lowering cortisol levels, the hormone linked to stress, meditation helps employees manage pressure more effectively. A study conducted by the University of

Massachusetts Medical School found that workplace mindfulness programs led to around a 20% reduction in stress levels and an increase in job satisfaction among employees.

In addition to stress relief, meditation sharpens focus and concentration. Regular practice trains the mind to stay present, minimizing distractions and boosting productivity. Employees who meditate often find themselves more attentive and efficient, leading to fewer errors and improved work output. This enhanced clarity also nurtures creativity and problem-solving skills, as a relaxed and open mind is more adept at generating innovative ideas and making well-considered decisions.

Meditation also plays a crucial role in emotional regulation. By increasing self-awareness, it helps individuals manage their emotions better, reducing workplace conflicts and improving interpersonal relationships. This heightened emotional intelligence not only aids in better communication but also fosters a supportive team environment, enhancing overall collaboration and cohesion.

Moreover, the benefits of meditation extend to job satisfaction and engagement. Employees who practice meditation tend to experience higher morale and a greater sense of fulfilment at work. This positive shift in attitude contributes to a healthier workplace culture, where satisfaction and loyalty thrive. Healthier employees, in turn, contribute to a reduction in absenteeism and burnout, creating a more resilient workforce.

Incorporating meditation into the workday is more than a personal advantage, it's a catalyst for organizational success. By improving focus, creativity, and emotional balance, meditation cultivates a thriving, productive, and harmonious work environment. As more organizations recognize these benefits, they are integrating meditation into their wellness programs, paving the way for a more balanced and effective workplace.

Meditation and self-awareness

At its core, meditation is a journey into the depths of one's own consciousness. It provides a means to explore and understand the true nature of the self beyond the superficial layers of identity. Through practices like self-inquiry and mindfulness, individuals can uncover a sense of inner clarity and self-realization. Many spiritual traditions view meditation as a way to transcend the ego, the sense of self that is often tied to desires, fears, and personal identity. Meditation offers powerful benefits, helping to cultivate a deeper sense of self-awareness and inner peace.

In the next chapter, we'll dive into how this heightened awareness can supercharge your performance at work, allowing you to manage your emotions and reactions more effectively. But first self-awareness must be honed and strengthened. Meditation sharpens your ability to spot recurring patterns in your thinking, feeling, and behaving.

Recognizing these patterns can empower you to choose healthier reactions. With time, meditation reveals the triggers that provoke certain emotional or behavioural responses, giving you a chance to pause and redirect.

Some types of meditation forms that can increase your self-awareness are breathwork or body scan meditations. Focusing on the breath or sensations keeps you grounded in the present moment, making you more aware of your immediate experiences rather than being lost in past regrets or future anxieties.

By creating space between your thoughts and your identity, you can better understand that thoughts are transient and don't define you. By consistently practicing mindfulness, you can form new neural pathways that support your self-awareness.

How to start

In this digital area, we are super fortunate to have access to a whole array of meditation videos, podcasts or books. You can find a multitude of these meditation guides online, to help walk you through how it is done.

A couple of techniques you can apply to kick-start the process are:

o Mentally scanning the body from head to toe, noticing tension, pain, or other sensations.
o Releasing tension in each area as you bring awareness to it.
o Sitting in a specific posture (e.g., lotus or half-lotus) with a straight spine.
o Focusing on the breath or observing thoughts without engagement.
o Mentally scanning the body from head to toe, noticing tension, pain, or other sensations.
o Releasing tension in each area as you bring awareness to it.
o Mentally scanning the body from head to toe, noticing tension, pain, or other sensations.
o Releasing tension in each area as you bring awareness to it.

Recommended read: *The Power of Now* has become a modern spiritual classic, influencing millions worldwide. It's a book that challenges readers to step outside of their conditioned ways of thinking and experience life as it truly is, one moment at a time. The book resonates with people from all walks of life because it offers a universal solution to everyday struggles: a shift in perspective. It's not about changing your circumstances but changing how you relate to them.

Finding ways to be present

You might question "how do I quiet my mind?" and "how long should I be doing this for?". There is no one size fits all solution for everyone, but we can all start by sitting in our present moment more intently. At work this might mean, taking a step back when you feel you stress levels rise. During a stressful meeting, instead of overthinking or planning your next response, focus on the sensation of your breath, how it enters your nostrils and fills your lungs. Feel the calm that comes from grounding yourself in the present through each inhale and exhale.

Use single tasking as a way to enter a 'focus flow' state. If you're working on a project, avoid checking emails or scrolling social media simultaneously. Focus entirely on the task at hand, appreciating the process instead of rushing toward completion. When moving from one activity to another, such as leaving work or arriving home, pause for a moment. Take a deep breath, notice your surroundings, and consciously shift your focus to the present before diving into the next task.

Take a walk and notice the world around you; the rustling of leaves, the chirping of birds, or the feeling of the ground beneath your feet. Instead of letting your mind drift, engage fully with the sights, sounds, and smells of your surroundings. Engage fully in your interactions as much as you can.

While talking to a friend or loved one, give them your full attention. Instead of planning your reply, listen deeply to their words, tone, and emotions. Notice their expressions and connect to the present moment by being fully there with them.

During a meal, pause before eating to notice the aroma and colours of your food. Take small bites, chew slowly, and savour the flavours and textures. Avoid distractions like your phone or TV and experience the joy of eating mindfully. By incorporating these small yet intentional practices into your daily life, you can train your mind to remain anchored in the present, finding peace and fulfilment in each moment.

12 Ways to minimise your triggers

"When awareness is brought to an emotion, power is brought to your life."
– Tara Meyer Robson

Difficult people

One of the biggest challenges many of us face is feeling triggered by colleagues or managers, or even our loved ones at home. While it's crucial to limit time around difficult people, sometimes exposure is unavoidable. Many of us find ourselves irritated by our colleagues for various reasons, often due to poor management practices and ineffective communication.

Offences like extreme micromanagement, stifle creativity and signal a lack of trust, which leaves employees feeling frustrated and undervalued. Similarly, favouritism, taking credit for others' work, and imposing unrealistic demands all create dysfunction in the workplace. These behaviours erode trust, limit productivity, and turn the workplace into a source of irritation rather than a space for collaboration and growth.

Navigating workplace dynamics can sometimes feel like balancing on a high wire, but there are ways to make it easier. Whether you're preparing to join a new team or dealing with a toxic situation in your current role, there are strategies to help you manage effectively while safeguarding your emotional well-being. You can start by identifying your triggers and finding ways to manage stress. Once you've regained a sense of control, you can adopt practical coping mechanisms to deflect or neutralize toxic behaviours.

It's important to remember that struggling with difficult colleagues isn't a sign of weakness or impatience. It is simply part of the complex nature of working closely with different people. Understanding why people act the way they do can help to shift your perspective. Often, difficult behaviour stems from personal troubles, unresolved patterns or experiences they carry. Their negativity weighs heaviest on themselves, far more than it does on you.

Truly happy people don't try to exert control, tear others down or create unnecessary drama; they lift others up and thrive in harmony. By keeping this in mind, you can approach workplace challenges with a greater sense of empathy, resilience, and inner peace. Self-reflection is key to understanding your triggers and evaluating whether these stem from internal perceptions rather than the external. Sometimes, what feels toxic might actually be very manageable with a shift in mindset.

Often, if you move to a new job without addressing your prior triggers, you may find yourself facing the same issues again and again. This is because all workplaces come with diverse personalities.

That said, it's also vital to recognize when a work environment is draining and becoming genuinely harmful. Work on recognising when to move on, in order to protect your well-being.

Before starting a new job

Before joining a company, it's crucial to get a clear sense of the culture, team dynamics, and the role you're stepping into. One of the best ways to do this is by tapping into tools such as review platforms like Glassdoor, which offer honest, third-party insights from current and former employees. These sites often provide a behind-the-scenes look at company culture, management styles, and even specific feedback about the team or role you're considering.

Some platforms are tailored for specific audiences, such as women seeking workplaces that prioritize inclusivity, while others offer a more general overview. By exploring these diverse perspectives, you can gain valuable information to make a well-informed decision about whether the company aligns with your values and career goals.

o **Indeed:** offers company reviews alongside its job listings. Employees can rate their employers and share detailed reviews about their work experience, management, work-life balance, and salary information.

o **Fairygodboss:** is a review site tailored specifically for women, offering insights into companies' policies on gender equality, work-life balance, and maternity leave.

o **Comparably:** provides employee reviews with a strong focus on company culture and compensation. It also allows users to compare salaries across companies and industries.

o **InHerSight:** is another platform dedicated to women's workplace experiences, offering reviews on companies' support for women, including policies on maternity leave, flexible work, and career advancement.

Now imagine that, after carefully researching and selecting a company, you've made it to the interview stage. Congratulations! Now comes the pivotal moment where both you and the employer evaluate each other. While it's important to leave a positive impression on the hiring manager, it's equally crucial to be open about your values and what truly matters to you.

Confidence is key here, the right company will appreciate your authenticity and interest in their culture, while the wrong one will not, and that's perfectly okay. By being true to yourself, you're clearing the way for the right opportunity to come along. When it's your turn to ask questions, take full advantage of this moment to gather the insights you need.

However, keep your questions intentional and concise, focusing on what truly matters to you. Remember, an interview is a two-way conversation, it's as much about discovering if the company fits you as it is about proving you're the right fit for them. Any standard, vague questions designed to impress the interviewer on how intelligent you are might score you a few points, but they are not going to give you the insights you need. Consider relevant and specific questions, such as:

o **What qualities do the most successful team members have in common?** This question helps you understand what values the team truly prioritizes. For example, if top performers are recognized for being highly organized, structured, and methodical, it might indicate that more fluid traits like flexibility and creativity aren't as valued within the team. This insight can help you determine if your strengths align with what the team rewards.

o **How does the team celebrate successes or recognize achievements?** This question can reveal whether the team values shared celebrations and connection or if they focus primarily on a no-frills personal reward, through mechanisms such as year-end bonuses. If you're someone who prefers straightforward recognition and a generous bonus, this might be a great fit. However, if you thrive in environments where achievements are celebrated with team outings or social events (e.g. a team ski-trip or private concert) a team that's more transactional in its approach may feel disconnected to you. There will be teams on both ends of the spectrum and some that land in the middle, so knowing what you prefer is crucial.

○ **Can you describe a typical day or week for someone on this team, and how does the team communicate and collaborate?** The interviewer should provide a clear picture of your role, the projects you'll tackle, and how often the team meets. If the answers are vague, it could be a red flag that they're just looking to fill a position without fully defining the role. This lack of clarity might mean you end up with tasks no one else wants, without clear direction. It can signal that you are joining a team that is in the midst of chaos, with a high workload and long hours, due to a lack of role boundaries and defined responsibilities. While this might be worth the risk for a company's prestige or if there are other factors that appeal to you, it is still something to consider carefully during the onboarding process.

○ **What is the staff turnover like?** This is a good indicator as to the employee satisfaction, if they have a lot of long term, loyal employees it is likely because they are being treated well and remunerated fairly. In contrast, high stress teams with a toxic culture tend to have a very high staff turnover and little reward for excessive work hours.

Toxicity in your current job

If you are already in a workplace with an unrewarding culture, then you can start to apply methods to mitigate the time spent in toxic situations and also take steps to improve your outlook. Navigating a toxic workplace requires a strategic approach to safeguard your well-being and find effective solutions. Start by pinpointing the core issues causing the toxicity and evaluate how they impact your job satisfaction and mental health. Setting clear personal boundaries and limiting exposure to negative influences can help you maintain balance.

Ultimately, the goal in any career is to be either learning or earning. So first you should assess if one of these is still taking place, before you consider moving jobs or teams, purely because of difficult colleagues. If you are developing an expertise in an area and increasing your earnings each year rightly so, then the role you are in might be perfect for your progression. If you are instead learning new things frequently in your role, garnering transferrable skills and industry specific insights, then again it might be worth holding on to this role for longer.

Focus on your professional growth by enhancing your skills and staying positive about aspects of your job that you enjoy. If the toxic environment remains persistent and you are neither earning or learning, then consider exploring other job opportunities or planning a strategic exit.

Protecting your mental health is essential, so seek professional help if needed and practice stress management techniques. Ultimately, maintaining resilience and perspective will help you navigate through the challenges and make informed decisions about your career.

How to reframe for specific examples

Start by shifting the way you approach your interactions with others. Stoicism teaches us to focus on what we can control, our thoughts, actions, and reactions, while accepting what lies beyond our influence. This mindset is invaluable in managing negativity, allowing you to maintain your inner peace regardless of external circumstances. At a deeper level, it's important to remember that we're all just humans, shaped by the experiences and environments we've encountered.

Each person carries the imprint of their upbringing and the behaviours they've absorbed along the way. Some are more self-aware than others, but if those around you struggle to collaborate or show understanding, it's likely because they haven't yet unlocked that potential within themselves. Patience and empathy go a long way in navigating these dynamics, as we all evolve at different paces.

Let's consider some scenarios...

Micromanagers

Micromanagers can be incredibly frustrating because their behaviour often undermines trust, stifles creativity, and creates a stressful work environment. Micromanaging is often rooted in psychological factors that drive a person's need for control and perfectionism.

Consider minimising the impact to your work by:

o Have a candid conversation with your manager about your work style and the negative impact micromanagement has on your performance.

o Set a cadence for how often you will update your manager on the status of your work or goals, this alleviates the stress they experience when they don't feel up to date on where things are at. Provide them an overview and direct access to any work in progress, this can create trust that mitigates their tendency to micromanage.

o Clarify goals and expectations upfront. By understanding exactly what is required, you can proactively address concerns before they arise, reducing the need for constant oversight.

o Micromanagers may derive their self-worth from the success of their projects or teams. They might feel that they must be deeply involved in every aspect to ensure success, consider this when providing them with updates, i.e. provide some specific details as well as an overview when communicating with them.

Dismissive colleagues and managers

A manager might be dismissive of work in various ways, often leading to frustration and demotivation among team members. This might involve ignoring milestones, not providing feedback, or overlooking the importance of tasks that employees have worked hard on. They might avoid dealing with conflicts within the team, leaving employees to feel unsupported and unimportant. Managers who are insecure about their own leadership skills may dismiss their team's input as a way to avoid revealing their perceived inadequacies. They may feel that acknowledging others' ideas could expose their own lack of knowledge or experience.

Consider handling these impacts by:

o Bringing them in as a secondary owner to your great work. As frustrating as this is, if you directly report to this manager, they will be the ultimate approver of your projects and the subsequent rewards for good work. Mitigate their need to dull your shine, by incorporating them as a 'reviewer' alongside you as the 'preparer' to the outputs you are working on. Document key successes and suggest team wide communications to acknowledge completion of key milestones, all whilst including their name, to encourage that recognition out of them.

o These types of managers often lack empathy and understanding, of the hard work it takes to complete certain tasks and project. Detach yourself from the need of approval, whilst still pushing for the right recognition. Do this by honing in on what issues you are resolving and how you have improved on existing processes through the work you have completed. This draws their attention to the quality of your inputs.

Recommended read: *Toxic managers, subordinates and other difficult people. – Roy H.Lubit, M.D, Ph.D.* In this book, one striking example features a manager driven by a constant need for admiration, who dismisses others' contributions and reacts with hostility when their authority is challenged. This type of manager might belittle employees during meetings or take credit for their work, creating a toxic environment. To navigate such a situation, Lubit suggests a strategic approach to managing the narcissist's ego. He advises carefully choosing battles and framing feedback in a way that avoids triggering the boss's defensiveness. A key tactic is to preface suggestions with genuine compliments about the boss's achievements, which can soften resistance and open the door to more constructive dialogue.

Colleagues that don't deliver results

Another scenario described in the book by Roy H.Lubit, is that of a colleague who consistently agrees to tasks and deadlines but fails to deliver, offering weak excuses that lead to project delays and frustration. Lubit recommends directly addressing this passive-aggressive behaviour by setting clear expectations and following up in writing after meetings. This approach creates accountability and minimizes the colleague's ability to shirk responsibilities.

It's OK to leave!

Work dynamics can sometimes become so toxic that remaining in such an environment takes a toll on your mental health, self-esteem, and overall well-being. Whether it's due to poor communication, lack of respect, or unhealthy competition, these issues can create a hostile atmosphere that stifles growth and productivity. In such situations, it's crucial to prioritize your well-being and recognize when it's time to move on.

Choosing to leave a toxic workplace is not a sign of failure but a courageous step toward finding an environment where your values align with those of the organization and your skills are genuinely appreciated. By seeking a healthier and more supportive workplace, you give yourself the opportunity to thrive both personally and professionally.

13 Upskill and be open to change

"Give me six hours to chop down a tree and I will spend the first four sharpening the axe."
– Abraham Lincoln

Staying relevant

This quote emphasizes the importance of preparation and skill refinement before tackling a challenge. Developing your skills in the workplace can be a game-changer. When you sharpen your abilities, you naturally become more efficient, able to handle complex projects with ease and delivering results that stand out. This not only enhances your productivity but also puts you on the radar for promotions and new career opportunities.

In today's fast-paced workplace, staying on top of your skills gives you a real edge, it provides job security and keeps you adaptable in a sea of shifting technologies and evolving roles. But it's not just about professional growth. Beyond career advancement, skill development brings a deep sense of confidence and personal fulfilment. As you grow, you'll find yourself not just keeping up with the workplace demands but thriving in them, ready to take on new challenges and step into leadership roles.

Whether you're aiming for a promotion or exploring a new career path, skill refinement isn't just about professional growth, it's the key to unlocking your full potential.

Ursula Burns' rise from intern to the CEO of Xerox is an extraordinary example of how upskilling and determination can shatter boundaries. Starting her journey in an entry-level role, she saw the power of education and earned a master's degree in mechanical engineering from Columbia University. Armed with technical expertise and a deep understanding of Xerox's inner workings, she championed innovation and rose through the ranks, ultimately making history as the first Black woman to lead a Fortune 500 company. Burns' story is a powerful reminder that with a commitment to growth, there are no limits to what you can achieve.

Start upskilling

Upskilling involves intentionally improving your knowledge and abilities to stay competitive and grow in your career. It can be about levelling up your existing talents or diving into fresh, uncharted topics. Here are some effective ways to upskill:

- Online Courses and Certifications: Platforms like Coursera, Udemy, and LinkedIn Learning offer courses in various fields, allowing you to learn at your own pace and earn certifications that boost your credentials.

o Attend Workshops and Seminars: In-person or virtual workshops and industry conferences provide a great opportunity to learn new skills, network with professionals, and stay updated on the latest trends in your field.

o Leverage Company Resources: Many employers offer training programs, mentorship opportunities, or skill development initiatives. Take advantage of these resources to grow in your current role while preparing for future opportunities.

o Join Professional Communities: Being part of a professional network, like LinkedIn groups or industry-specific organizations, can expose you to valuable knowledge, best practices, and potential mentors.

o Self-Learning: Books, podcasts, and free online resources are a great way to deepen your understanding of a subject. Commit to daily or weekly learning sessions to steadily build your skills.

o Practice and Experiment: Apply your new skills in real-world situations. Whether it's through side projects, volunteering, or taking on a new project area at work, practicing what you've learned solidifies your abilities.

- o Get a Mentor: A mentor can offer guidance, advice, and feedback as you upskill. They can help you focus on the right areas and provide insight based on their experience.

- o Soft Skills Development: Don't overlook soft skills like communication, leadership, and time management. These are often just as important as technical skills and can be developed through reading, feedback, and practice.

Be open to new opportunities

Even if you're content in your current role, keeping an eye on new job opportunities is highly beneficial. The job market is always evolving, and staying in the loop helps you stay informed about industry trends, competitive salaries, and the skills in demand. By staying proactive, you'll be ready to seize a better opportunity when it comes along, whether it's for career growth, improved work-life balance, or a role that feels more fulfilling.

Exploring your options also gives you a stronger sense of control over your career, helping you stay adaptable and avoid stagnation in a world of constant change. In the end, staying open to new possibilities isn't just about moving up; it's about aligning your career with your ever-evolving goals and aspirations. Exploring other opportunities can even deepen your appreciation for your current role and company.

By benchmarking the perks and benefits you enjoy, you'll gain a clearer picture of what sets your workplace apart, highlighting the unique positives that might be easy to overlook. Regularly engaging with the job market keeps you informed and ready, giving you a competitive edge whether you're negotiating with your current employer or contemplating a future move. Embarking on job applications and taking interviews can be a savvy move to stay ahead in your career, even if you don't take the new role. These interactions also expand your professional network, potentially unlocking future opportunities and connections.

Consider interviewing externally at least once a year, just to be able to benchmark your 'market value' at a similar role or see if you've gained enough experience to take a step up in a higher position. It's also a fantastic confidence booster and an opportunity to refine your verbal communication skills for professional settings. It's the perfect practice ground to sharpen how you present your ideas and articulate your value. Plus, the feedback you receive can sharpen your skills and enhance your resume for the future.

Navigating an internal move

A fresh start doesn't always mean jumping ship to a new company. Sometimes, the change you are craving could be as simple as switching teams, moving to a new department, or even relocating to another office in a new city.

Making an internal move can breathe new life into your career. If you're craving change, this shift can offer a fresh perspective and reignite your passion for your work. It's also a powerful way to boost your visibility across the organisation, highlighting your adaptability and dedication to the company.

Great leaders often rise to the top by immersing themselves in different areas of a business, gaining the well-rounded expertise needed to make transformative decisions. Mary Barra, CEO of General Motors, started off as a student in engineering. She worked across HR, manufacturing, and product development, building a deep understanding of the company's operations.

Similarly, Doug McMillon, CEO of Walmart, began unloading trucks in a distribution centre and climbed through roles in merchandising, logistics, and store management, giving him unparalleled insight into every aspect of the business. These leaders show that stepping out of silos cultivates the strategic thinking needed to steer companies to extraordinary success.

Transitioning internally comes with unique perks, like already being familiar with the company's culture and operations, so you can dive into your new role without the steep learning curve. You're also already clued up on all of the systems and tools, a significant advantage that saves you the time and effort. It also comes with the opportunity to strengthen your professional network.

By building deeper relationships with colleagues and expanding your connections within the company, you open the door to exciting future opportunities. Plus, staying with your company can provide a sense of stability. It provides opportunities to build new skills, all while staying grounded in a workplace you know and feel confident with. These moves often allow you to keep your existing benefits, seniority, and sometimes even lead to an increase in base salary, making the move both practical and advantageous.

Connecting with mentors

A professional mentor is someone who offers guidance, support, and insight to help you navigate your career path. They bring years of experience and wisdom, providing invaluable advice on everything from decision-making to overcoming challenges. A mentor acts as a sounding board, helping you identify your strengths, areas for improvement, and opportunities for growth.

Selecting the right mentors can be a transformative step in your personal and professional journey. To make sure you find the perfect match, start by clarifying what you want to achieve through mentorship, whether it's accelerating your career, mastering specific skills, or fostering personal growth. With a clear vision of your goals, look for mentors who have are successful in the areas that resonate most with you.

Seek out mentors who are respected in their field, their acclaim can be a good sign of their effectiveness. Make sure to diversify your mentors as much as you can, different perspectives can offer unique insights. Compatibility is key, so look for mentors whose values and communication style resonate with yours.

Passion and empathy are key qualities to look for in a mentor. Seek someone who is genuinely invested in your growth and excited to support you. Consider their availability; you'll want someone who genuinely has the time to guide you. Keep in mind that mentoring should be a two-way exchange, where both you and your mentor can learn and grow together. A strong mentor-mentee relationship thrives on mutual respect and understanding.

By choosing mentors who embody great qualities, you'll create a powerful, supportive network that not only helps you reach your goals but also encourages you to thrive.

Keep score of your wins

The appraisal process in the workplace, often referred to as a performance review, is a systematic approach used by organizations to assess employee performance, provide feedback, and plan for future development. Continuous feedback is encouraged to address issues or recognize achievements in real-time, rather than waiting until the formal review.

Performance appraisals often play a critical role in decisions about salary increases, bonuses, and promotions. Employees who perform well are generally rewarded, while those who need improvement may receive support such as coaching or additional training. This is why it is critical to perform a self-appraisal before your manager discussion.

Keep track of all of your projects, weekly progress and every small win. If you receive positive feedback at the end of a meeting, via an email, or even a chat message, take screenshots and notes. Document these regularly, ideally bi-weekly or at least monthly in order to have solid evidence of your performance and the positive impact you've had to those you work with. A great way to keep this all handy is to have a file or folder (or using an notes app like OneNote) where you can store all of these evidences to refer to this when writing up your personal appraisal.

Consider keeping track of the following:

o   Identify your key 'customers': people you worked with that relied on your outputs, what feedback have they given and what was the outcome of your delivery to them?

o   How have you communicated with managers and colleagues, what has been your style and frequency? Consider what the positives of your communication methods have been.

o Avoid dwelling too much on areas for improvement. It is important to still openly recognise these, but keep the focus positive by redirecting attention to your strengths. For instance, if you missed a deadline due to waiting for crucial data or deciding to refine the output for accuracy, highlight how you handled the situation. Emphasize how you prioritized quality over speed, demonstrating your commitment to delivering the best possible result. Shift the conversation to how your strengths—like attention to detail and commitment to excellence—shaped your decision.

The appraisal process isn't just a gateway to promotions and better pay, it's a powerful opportunity to reflect on your achievements and recognize the value you bring to your workplace. It's a moment to celebrate your contributions, remind yourself of your strengths, and reaffirm your impact, fuelling your confidence and motivation for the future.

14 Work less hours

"Being busy is not the same as being productive. Productivity is about getting the most important things done." – Tim Ferris

The burnout badge of honour

Over the past century, the evolution of productivity tools has revolutionized the way we work, organize, and manage our time. In the early 20th century, productivity relied on manual methods; paper planners, physical ledgers, and mechanical time trackers. Work was tangible, but progress was slow and labour-intensive. Everything changed with the advent of personal computers.

Digital calendars, task management software, and early project management tools streamlined processes, reducing manual effort and bringing structure to workflows. Cloud-based platforms like Google Workspace and Microsoft Teams enabled real-time collaboration, instant communication, and seamless file sharing, connecting teams regardless of location. Today, we're witnessing yet another leap forward with AI-driven tools and automation. These technologies analyse data, optimize workflows, and take over repetitive tasks, empowering us to focus on high-value work.

Productivity is no longer static, it's dynamic, intuitive, and continuously adapting to the fast-paced demands of the modern workforce. As technology advances, the way we work will keep evolving, pushing the boundaries of what's possible.

Despite the incredible advancements in modern technology designed to simplify our lives, many people are still working longer hours and grappling with burnout. We now have tools that allow for instant communication, task automation, and the flexibility to work from anywhere, yet the pressure to always be "on" has only intensified. Instead of giving us more time, technology often dissolves the boundaries between work and personal life. Emails, notifications, and messages follow us everywhere, pinging at all hours, demanding attention.

The result? Many of us find ourselves perpetually connected, working overtime without even realizing it, and struggling to carve out moments to breathe. Our brains, much like a finely tuned engine, aren't designed to run at full throttle indefinitely. As time ticks by, a mix of physiological and psychological forces begins to work against us. Fatigue creeps in, wrapping us in that foggy-headed haze that makes even simple tasks feel Herculean.

This isn't us underperforming, this is just our biology. Your brain is signalling that its energy reserves are depleting and it needs a break.

When we ignore these signals, stress and burnout take over, making matters worse. We become stuck in a rigid, tunnel-vision mindset, unable to see beyond the immediate task at hand. We're spinning our wheels but going nowhere. Understanding these limits isn't a weakness; it's a strength. Recognizing that our productivity isn't infinite gives us permission to pause, recharge, and return stronger. The most productive thing we can do is mastering the art of balancing focus and rest.

Many workaholics wear their 12-hour days like a badge of honour, convinced they're achieving twice as much. But science paints a very different picture. Multiple studies show that the number of hours a person can work productively is limited, and working longer hours often leads to diminishing returns. This relentless grind doesn't lead to better results; it leads to burnout. Over time, those stuck in this cycle aren't producing high-quality work, they're simply running on empty, with their brainpower overheating. The key isn't working more, but working smarter and allowing your mind to recharge.

Productivity Decline After 50 Hours per Week

A fascinating study from Stanford University uncovered a surprising truth: productivity sharply declines after working 50 hours per week! Strikingly, individuals who push themselves to 70 hours don't achieve significantly more than those working around 55 hours.

The extra hours you think are boosting your output may actually be wasted effort. Interestingly, the sweet spot for productivity tends to be around 40 hours per week. Beyond this threshold, the returns diminish quickly, and the risks increase.

Working beyond 50 hours a week can severely affect cognitive function, leading to a rise in mistakes, poor decision-making, and burnout. Research shows that extended hours not only diminish concentration but also impair memory, problem-solving, and creativity. When fatigue sets in, the brain struggles to process information effectively, which increases the likelihood of errors.

Pushing yourself to work long hours might feel like the path to success, but the toll it takes on your health tells a very different story. According to research from the World Health Organization (WHO), consistently working around 60 hours or more per week is linked to a significantly higher risk of heart disease and stroke. In fact, the WHO reports that overwork is a major contributor to premature deaths globally.

In Japan, the term "karoshi" refers to death from overwork, highlighting the severe consequences of excessive working hours. In India, as recently as 2024, a 26-year-old executive at Ernst & Young died due to extreme overwork. This incident caught the attention of the public and prompted Indian states to draft stricter workplace regulations to protect workers from excessive work schedules and unjust dismissals.

In the United States, the banking sector has also faced scrutiny over employee overwork, following the death of a 35-year-old. JPMorgan Chase and Bank of America have since implemented measures to limit work hours and enhance time tracking systems.

The takeaway is clear, working harder and for longer hours doesn't always mean working smarter. It's not about putting in the longest shifts. Taking breaks, setting boundaries, and practicing self-care are key to sustaining peak performance and long-term success.

Our 90-minute cognitive focus span

Our brains are amazing, but they're not built for endless focus. Cognitive science reveals that after about 90 minutes of deep, uninterrupted work, our ability to maintain peak concentration begins to wane. This phenomenon ties back to a natural biological cycle called the ultradian rhythm, which governs our energy levels and mental focus throughout the day. When we push past this natural threshold without a pitstop for rest, our brain's energy reserves begin to deplete, leading to reduced performance, mental fatigue, and errors.

The good news? The key to sustaining productivity lies in knowing when to pause and then return to work. Research shows that taking breaks, especially structured ones, can recharge our mental batteries and restore focus.

Techniques like the Pomodoro Technique are grounded in this science, breaking work into manageable intervals (such as 25 minutes of focus followed by a 5-minute break) to optimize efficiency and stave off burnout.

Even for longer periods of concentration, such as 90-minute work cycles, incorporating a 15-20 minutes of restorative break afterward has been shown to sharpen attention, boost creativity, and improve overall productivity. Activities like taking a short walk, stretching, meditating, or simply stepping away from your desk can reset your mind and help you return with renewed energy.

By aligning your workflow with your brain's natural rhythms, you're not just working smarter, you're setting yourself up for long-term success, creativity, and satisfaction in your tasks. So, embrace the rhythm, and let those breaks become your productivity secret weapon!

The 4-Hour Rule of Deep Work

Unlocking peak productivity means entering the coveted flow state, that mental sweet spot where distractions fade, time seems to dissolve, and your work feels effortless yet deeply purposeful. In this state, you're not just checking tasks off a list; you're creating, innovating, and solving problems with laser-like focus. But here's the catch: achieving and sustaining this level of intense concentration has its limits.

Dr. K. Anders Ericsson, a pioneering neuroscientist known for his research on elite performers, discovered a fascinating truth: the human brain can only sustain deep, focused work for about four hours a day before fatigue sets in. Whether it's a virtuoso violinist practicing for a recital or an athlete training for gold, Ericsson found that top-tier performance hinges not on working endlessly but on working strategically. This research, popularized by Cal Newport's influential book Deep Work, underscores a vital principle: the quality of your focus outweighs the quantity of your hours.

Why only four hours? The brain, much like a muscle, requires rest after periods of intense exertion to perform at its best. Pushing beyond this threshold doesn't lead to better results, it leads to diminishing returns, mental exhaustion, and, ultimately, burnout. Interestingly, some of history's most brilliant minds instinctively structured their days around this rhythm. Charles Darwin, for instance, spent his mornings tackling the most challenging scientific problems, reserving the rest of the day for leisure, light work, or walks. Similarly, mathematician Henri Poincaré adhered to a schedule of short, focused work sessions to fuel his ground-breaking insights.

What kind of work fits into this four-hour window? High-impact, creative, and cognitively demanding tasks like problem-solving, writing, or deep strategizing. By dedicating this time to your most important work and protecting it from interruptions, you set the stage for extraordinary results.

Embrace this four-hour focus rule by prioritizing rest, planning your day around bursts of high-impact work, and letting your brain recharge in between. This isn't just about productivity, it's about finding a rhythm that fuels creativity, supports long-term success, and helps you work at your absolute best.

In essence, the concept of 4-hour deep work advocates for a disciplined approach to work, emphasizing the importance of concentrated effort and structured time management to achieve high-impact results:

o Focused Work Block: The core of this concept is dedicating a specific, uninterrupted period—usually about four hours—to dive into tasks that demand high levels of focus and mental effort. This time is set aside for activities like strategic planning, solving complex problems, or engaging in creative work where deep concentration is key.

o Minimized Distractions: To make the most of these four hours, it's crucial to block out distractions. This means silencing notifications, finding a quiet workspace, and using techniques to maintain focus. The aim is to create an environment where your mind can fully engage with the task, free from interruptions.

o Structured Time Management: Deep work often thrives within a structured routine. Many people schedule these four-hour blocks at their peak productivity time, ensuring they're alert and energized. This regularity helps build a habit and reinforces the benefits of focused, uninterrupted work.

o High-Value Outcomes: The idea is to focus on tasks that matter—those that lead to meaningful results or long-term progress. By dedicating time to deep work, individuals aim to produce high-quality output, making significant strides on important projects, rather than getting bogged down in low-impact tasks.

o Balancing Shallow Work: While deep work is critical, it's equally important to make room for shallow work—things like emails, meetings, and administrative duties. Good time management means creating space for these routine tasks without letting them interfere with your dedicated deep work sessions.

Online productivity tools

Embracing online productivity tools can transform the way you work, boosting efficiency and streamlining daily tasks. These powerful solutions give you instant access to your projects from any device, ensuring you have oversight that no matter where you are.

Features like real-time updates, and automation reduce time spent on repetitive tasks, freeing up mental energy for more strategic work. Organizational apps are at the forefront, revolutionizing the way we capture, store, and manage information. These digital tools go beyond simple note-taking by offering features like cloud synchronization, searchable databases, and multimedia integration, ensuring that important ideas and documents are always accessible.

Whether it's jotting down meeting notes, saving web clippings, or organizing research, apps like Evernote, Notion, and OneNote help users structure their thoughts efficiently. With so many options on the market, what do each of these really do and how can they benefit us:

o **Notion** – An all-in-one workspace for notes, databases, project management, and collaboration. It allows users to create structured workspaces with customizable templates for everything from personal to-do lists to complex team workflows. With features like drag-and-drop organization, embedded multimedia, and relational databases, Notion is perfect for professionals and teams looking for an adaptable workspace.

o **Asana** – A powerful task management and team collaboration platform to keep projects on track. It provides task assignments, progress tracking, timelines, and workflow automation to improve efficiency. Whether you're managing complex projects or daily todos, Asana helps you prioritize work, set deadlines, and streamline communication within teams.

○ **Evernote** – A note-taking and organization app designed for capturing ideas and managing information. With features like text notes, voice memos, web clippings, and document scanning, it's ideal for professionals, students, and creatives looking for a seamless way to organize their thoughts.

○ **Todoist** – A simple yet effective task management and to-do list app for personal and professional use. It simplifies task prioritization with features like due dates, recurring reminders, productivity tracking, and project sharing.

○ **OneNote** – A digital notebook that allows users to capture and organize notes, sketches, and ideas in an intuitive way. OneNote offers freeform organization, meaning you can type anywhere on a page, draw freely, or insert multimedia elements. It's a great tool for professionals and creatives who prefer a flexible and visual approach to note-taking.

By integrating any of these tools into your routine, you can work smarter and maximize productivity, helping you achieve more with less effort.

The future of work

Forward-thinking companies around the world are challenging traditional work norms and pioneering innovative approaches to boost productivity and employee well-being.

Experiments with reduced hours, like the four-day workweek, are showing remarkable results. Companies in the UK, Iceland, and New Zealand have discovered that working fewer hours doesn't mean getting less done.

In fact, shorter, more focused workweeks often lead to higher levels of productivity as employees adopt smarter habits, eliminate distractions, and prioritize meaningful outcomes over sheer time spent at a desk. The benefits extend beyond performance, employees report improved mental health, greater job satisfaction, and a healthier work-life balance, resulting in a workforce that is more energized and loyal. These successes underscore a powerful truth: when businesses prioritize efficiency and well-being, everyone wins. Sometimes, less truly is more.

In addition to reducing hours, many workplaces are rethinking how time is spent during the week. Techniques like "No-Meeting Fridays" or limiting unnecessary meetings have emerged as game-changing solutions to help employees reclaim their focus. Meetings, while useful for collaboration, often fragment the day and disrupt deep, concentrated work. By carving out meeting-free days, companies are giving their teams the uninterrupted space they need to think and deliver results. The outcome? Sharper focus, a notable boost in productivity, and a workforce that feels more engaged.

These initiatives are just the beginning of how businesses are tackling overwork. By leveraging productivity-enhancing technologies, they're automating mundane tasks and allowing employees to focus on what truly matters.

At the same time, they're shifting toward a results-driven culture, one that values quality of work over the number of hours logged. This evolving mindset is ushering in a modern era of work-life harmony where employees can perform at their best without sacrificing their well-being.

15 Align with your energy cycles

"The menstrual cycle is a powerful force that connects women to the earth and to each other." — Miranda Gray

The sun and the moon

The study of women's menstrual cycles has evolved significantly over the centuries. Early observations were often steeped in myth and superstition. Historically, many cultures observed that menstrual cycles often seemed to synchronize with lunar phases, leading to the association between the moon and menstruation. Ancient societies, including the Greeks and Native American tribes, often associated menstruation with lunar deities and rituals. This connection may stem from the fact that both the average menstrual cycle and the lunar cycle are roughly 28 days long, albeit they don't align perfectly.

The scientific exploration of menstruation began to gain traction in the 19th and early 20th centuries, as researchers like Thomas H. Huxley and others began to uncover the biological and hormonal underpinnings of the cycle. By the mid-20th century, advances in endocrinology and reproductive health led to a more comprehensive understanding of hormonal regulation, with ground breaking work on the role of oestrogen and progesterone.

The late 20th and early 21st centuries have seen a surge in research focusing on the impact of menstrual cycles on overall health, mood, and productivity, driven by a growing recognition of the importance of women's health issues in broader medical research. Today, the study of menstrual cycles continues to expand, incorporating new insights from endocrinology, psychology, and even technology to better understand and support women's well-being throughout their lives.

Our cycles as a super power

Our natural rhythm allows us to tap into different strengths at various times throughout the month, making us more adaptable, creative, and emotionally intelligent. These fluctuations give us a unique edge in handling diverse tasks, helping us approach challenges with flexibility and a well-rounded perspective. It's important to recognize that men, though they don't have a monthly cycle, experience their own hormonal fluctuations, just on a daily basis. Testosterone levels rise and fall throughout the day, leading to peaks of energy in the morning and dips by evening. This daily cycle means that, like women, men's energy and emotional states can shift in significant ways, though the timeline is much shorter.

While it's tempting to compare the two, it's an oversimplification to equate men's daily energy patterns with women's monthly cycles. Women typically experience several days of consistent energy flow, whether high or low,

Corporate Girl Wellness

that corresponds to different phases of their hormonal cycle. This allows for sustained bursts of creativity or focus over time. On the other hand, men's energy cycles typically play out in hours rather than days, just like the Sun, with a peak in the morning and a gradual decline as the day progresses.

Overall, both genders experience natural rhythms that shape their performance. Women's cycles offer prolonged periods of high energy or introspection, while men's daily fluctuations lead to shorter bursts of intense focus. Understanding these differences helps highlight the unique ways our bodies interact with the demands of work, showing that both men and women bring dynamic energy to the table, just across different time-frames.

It's crucial to recognize that women do not struggle with work demands simply because they're in their menstrual phase. Just as a man might find it hard to focus when his energy and hormones dip, a woman can also push through and stay committed to her goals, even during the more challenging phases of her cycle. Both genders experience these fluctuations, and while these cycles may differ, they don't determine our ability to perform at work.

Managing your outputs during your cycle

Women's menstrual cycles can actually offer unique advantages in the workplace when understood and leveraged effectively.

161

Our energy levels often align with the four phases of the cycle, provided we have a regular cycle and balanced hormones. By syncing with these natural rhythms, we can optimize productivity during each phase.

1. During the **menstrual phase** (Days 1-5), fatigue can set in as the body sheds its lining.
2. As oestrogen rises in the **follicular phase** (Days 6-14), energy, mood, and focus improve, making it a great time to tackle big tasks.
3. **Ovulation** (Day 14) marks the peak of energy, with hormones at their highest, boosting confidence and drive.
4. In the **luteal phase** (Days 15-28), rising progesterone may cause a dip in energy, leading to tiredness and reduced motivation.

Track your cycle using a menstrual app or calendar to gain insight into your unique energy patterns. This helps you anticipate when you'll feel most energized or when you might need extra rest. If you have flexible working hours, use this to your advantage by structuring your schedule around your natural rhythm.

Look into your workplace's flexible work policies and, if possible, request adjustments that support your productivity. This isn't about working less, it's about working better. By aligning your tasks with your energy levels, you can sustain peak performance throughout the month. Additionally, syncing your workouts and nutrition with your cycle can further enhance your overall well-being and optimize both energy and productivity.

This chapter is here to inform and inspire, but it's not a substitute for professional medical or nutritional advice. Before making any changes to your lifestyle around your menstruation, be sure to consult a qualified expert.

Menstrual Phase (around days 1-6)

Some women may experience symptoms such as cramps, fatigue, bloating, and mood changes due to the drop-in hormone levels. However, as the menstrual phase progresses and the body starts preparing for the next cycle, energy levels and mood may gradually begin to improve. During the menstrual phase, women can tap into their body's natural rhythms to boost productivity in a more mindful, sustainable way.

This is a time to honour rest and reflection, giving space for strategic planning and big-picture thinking. By focusing on the essentials and streamlining your workflow, you can stay efficient without draining your energy. Setting clear boundaries and communicating your needs creates a supportive environment, while self-care practices recharge and keep you centred.

By scheduling more demanding tasks for later in the cycle, you preserve balance and optimize productivity. Use this time to focus on low-energy activities, like organizing your workspace or mapping out your upcoming tasks, ensuring you stay on track while respecting your body's needs.

o Administrative Tasks: Organize your inbox, clear out files, schedule meetings, and handle routine paperwork. These tasks don't require intense focus but still contribute to productivity.

o Reflection and Planning: This phase can be a great time for introspection. Use it to review progress on long-term goals, reflect on what's working and what isn't, and plan your upcoming projects.

o Creative Brainstorming: While energy may be low, your mind can be more open and receptive to new ideas. Brainstorming and coming up with creative concepts or solutions that don't require immediate action can be productive and feel less draining.

o Email and Communication: Responding to emails, catching up on messages, or drafting communications that don't need immediate response can be ideal. This allows you to stay engaged without requiring heavy mental exertion.

o Review and Editing: If you need to go over reports, documents, or presentations, this is a good time for editing and refining. It allows you to stay productive while not demanding high energy levels for creation or analysis.

During the menstrual phase, your body is doing important work, and it's essential to nurture it with the right foods to ease symptoms and support your well-being. This is a time to listen to your body and choose exercises that honour its energy levels.

By fuelling your body properly and embracing movement that feels right for you, you can help maintain balance and comfort.

Here are some anecdotal tips during this time:

o Leafy Greens: Spinach, kale, and other dark leafy greens are rich in iron, which can help replenish the iron lost during menstruation and combat fatigue.

o Nuts and Seeds: Almonds, walnuts, flaxseeds, and chia seeds are great sources of magnesium and omega-3 fatty acids, which can help reduce bloating and improve mood.

o Lean Proteins: Chicken, turkey, tofu, and legumes provide the protein necessary for energy and help stabilize blood sugar levels.

o Whole Grains: Foods like quinoa, brown rice, and oats are high in fibre and can help regulate digestion, which can be beneficial for managing bloating and constipation.

o Fatty Fish: Salmon, mackerel, and sardines are rich in omega-3 fatty acids, which can help reduce inflammation and alleviate menstrual cramps.

o Dark Chocolate: In moderation, dark chocolate can satisfy cravings and provide magnesium, which can help with mood swings and cramps.

o Gentle Cardio: Activities like walking, cycling, or light jogging can help boost your mood and energy levels without putting too much strain on your body.

o Yoga: Yoga can be particularly beneficial during your period. Gentle poses and stretches can alleviate cramps, reduce bloating, and promote relaxation. Poses like child's pose, cat-cow, and gentle twists can be very soothing.
o Stretching: Gentle stretching can help relieve muscle tension and improve circulation, which can ease cramps and discomfort.

Follicular Phase (around days 6-14)

Creativity is at its peak during this phase. As oestrogen levels rise, they supercharge your creativity and problem-solving skills, making it the perfect time to dive into brainstorming sessions and tackle complex projects. You may find yourself overflowing with fresh ideas and innovative solutions, ready to take on whatever challenges lie ahead.

With heightened motivation and a surge of energy, this period is ideal for setting bold goals, pushing through difficult tasks, and seizing new growth opportunities. It's a prime moment to embrace strategic planning and take on high-energy activities that will propel you forward in your career.

o Plan ambitious projects
o Set clear goals
o Engage in collaborative work
o Spent time learning new skills
o Tackle high-energy tasks

As your body experiences a natural surge in energy, it's the perfect time to fuel up with nutrient-dense foods that support your body's increased vitality. Incorporate workouts that challenge your body, this is the phase to start to push yourself with more intense exercises like strength training or cardio. The heightened levels of oestrogen give you the endurance and motivation to tackle ambitious goals, so embrace this time to make strides both physically and mentally.

o Incorporate protein-rich foods such as; lean meats, fish, eggs, and legumes to support energy levels and muscle function.
o Eat a variety of colourful fruits and veggies to boost vitamins and antioxidants. Citrus fruits and leafy greens are particularly beneficial.
o Include healthy fats such as; avocados, nuts, seeds, and olive oil to support brain health and overall well-being.
o Stay on top of hydrating foods, such as cucumbers and watermelon, to support optimal bodily functions.
o Engage in high-intensity interval training (HIIT), running, or cycling to take advantage of your increased energy levels and improve cardiovascular health.
o Focus on weightlifting or bodyweight exercises to build muscle and enhance overall strength.
o Participate in group fitness classes or team sports, where your enhanced social energy and motivation can make the experience more enjoyable and effective.

Ovulatory Phase (around days 14-21)

During ovulation, women often find their social skills and verbal fluency at an all-time high, making it the perfect moment to shine in communication and collaboration. Your communication skills and charisma are at their peak, making it the perfect time to network, pitch ideas, or lead projects. This phase is ideal for team meetings, networking events, and any projects that require strong interpersonal connections.

With boosted confidence and assertiveness from elevated oestrogen levels, it's also an excellent time to step into leadership roles, tackle high-stakes decisions, and manage key tasks with newfound influence. Embrace this period to leverage your enhanced abilities and make a significant impact in your professional and personal endeavours:

- o Tackle high-stakes tasks
- o Engage in networking
- o Leam team efforts
- o Set and review goals
- o Participate in public speaking
- o Celebrate achievements

During the ovulatory phase, you're at your peak, energy is high, focus is sharp, and confidence soars. Keep fuelling your body with foods that support your heightened energy, such as lean proteins, antioxidant-packed vegetables, and healthy fats that help sustain that natural boost. When it comes to exercise, this is the phase to go for intensity.

Take advantage of your body's increased stamina with challenging workouts like HIIT or strength training. Try to maximize this powerhouse phase.

o Focus on lean proteins, incorporate chicken, fish, tofu, and legumes to support muscle function and sustained energy levels.

o Keep carbohydrates complex: opt for whole grains like brown rice, quinoa, and oats to provide steady energy and maintain focus.

o Increase antioxidant rich foods, eat plenty of berries, leafy greens, and colourful vegetables to support overall health.

o High-Intensity Interval Training (HIIT), take advantage of your peak energy with intense cardio workouts that boost endurance and metabolism.

o Engage in weightlifting or bodyweight exercises to build muscle and maintain physical strength.

o Incorporate dynamic cardio, participate in activities like running, cycling, or dance classes that utilize your increased stamina and enthusiasm.

o Join classes or team sports that leverage your sociability and motivation, making workouts more enjoyable and effective.

o Enjoy outdoor exercise like hiking or sports, where your elevated mood and energy levels can enhance both performance and enjoyment.

Luteal Phase (Days 22-28):

During the luteal phase, your body's natural rhythm shifts, but this can be a time of precision. As your energy begins to dip, you may find that your focus sharpens, making it the perfect moment to dive into detail-oriented tasks that require careful planning, organization, and accuracy. This is when you can really thrive in meticulous projects, ensuring that every element is thoughtfully executed.

Hormonal changes during this phase also heighten emotional intelligence and empathy, allowing you to connect better with others. Your ability to understand and support colleagues becomes more intuitive, strengthening team dynamics and fostering a positive, collaborative work environment.

o Focus on Detail-Oriented Tasks: The luteal phase is a great time for tasks that require careful attention to detail. Use this period to tackle projects that need meticulous planning, organization, and accuracy.
o Prioritize Planning and Follow-Through: Utilize the heightened ability to plan and execute tasks. Focus on completing projects, refining work, and tying up loose ends during this phase.
o Enhance Team Collaboration: The hormonal changes during this phase can increase empathy and emotional intelligence. Use this time to strengthen team dynamics by being more attuned to colleagues' needs and fostering a supportive work environment.

o Schedule Thoughtful Meetings: Plan meetings that require deep listening, understanding, and collaborative problem-solving. Your enhanced emotional awareness can help in navigating complex interpersonal dynamics.

The luteal phase is a time to embrace mindfulness and self-compassion, as it can bring emotional challenges due to hormonal shifts. With fluctuating levels of progesterone and oestrogen, mood swings, irritability, anxiety, or even feelings of sadness may arise.

It's important to remember that these emotional shifts are a natural part of the cycle, so be gentle with yourself. It is a key time to communicate your needs to those around you. Whether it's asking for space, support, or simply a bit more understanding, sharing your needs can help alleviate tension.

Support your body during this phase with relaxation techniques and nourishing practices. Incorporate foods rich in mood-boosting nutrients, like omega-3 fatty acids, magnesium, and vitamin B6, which help support emotional stability. Stay hydrated, enjoy balanced meals, and allow yourself regular breaks to recharge. Gentle activities like yoga, meditation, or deep breathing can also help manage stress.

Embrace this phase as a time of self-care, using the right tools and practices to honour your body and mind.

o Uptake on complex carbohydrates: Foods like sweet potatoes, whole grains (brown rice, quinoa, oats), and legumes help stabilize blood sugar levels, reducing mood swings and energy crashes.

o Spinach, kale, and other leafy greens are rich in magnesium, which can help combat cramps, and alleviate mood swings.

o In addition to leafy greens, foods like dark chocolate, and almonds are excellent sources of magnesium, which can help alleviate PMS symptoms like irritability.

o Vitamin B6: Foods like chickpeas, bananas, and salmon are high in vitamin B6, which can help reduce symptoms of PMS by supporting hormone regulation.

o Staying hydrated is crucial. Herbal teas like chamomile or ginger can also help with bloating and soothe digestive discomfort.

o Yoga: Gentle yoga practices, especially restorative or yin yoga, can help reduce stress, ease tension, and improve flexibility. Focus on poses that support relaxation, such as forward bends, twists, and hip openers.

o Pilates: Pilates is great for maintaining core strength and flexibility without overly taxing the body. The controlled movements help improve posture and stability while being gentle on the joints.

o Stretching and Mobility Work: Incorporating a stretching routine or mobility exercises can help alleviate any stiffness or tension that might arise during the luteal phase, promoting relaxation and reducing discomfort.

Supportive workplace policies

Employers are increasingly recognizing the importance of supporting women's health needs, including those related to menstruation, as part of their commitment to fostering a balanced and healthy work environment. More companies are offering benefits like paid menstrual leave or mental health days, understanding that these practices not only support employee well-being but also contribute to long-term productivity and work-life harmony.

While there may not be specific laws addressing menstrual cycles, many countries provide broader legal rights to flexible working arrangements that can help women manage their health at work. For example, currently in the UK, employees with around 26 weeks of service can request flexible working hours. Although not specifically designed for menstrual health, this allows women to adjust their schedules and manage cycle-related challenges more effectively. Employers are required to consider such requests seriously and provide valid reasons if they are rejected.

In the U.S., while flexible working isn't a nationwide entitlement, many companies offer it as a benefit. Additionally, women may be entitled to time off under the Family and Medical Leave Act if menstruation leads to a serious health issue, ensuring they are supported during difficult times. Some countries, like Japan and Indonesia, have gone a step further, enacting laws that allow women to take leave during menstruation.

While these laws vary by region, they reflect a significant shift towards recognizing the real-world impact of menstrual health on work.

For women experiencing conditions like endometriosis or PCOS, which can cause severe menstrual symptoms, workplace accommodations may be available. These conditions are increasingly recognized as disabilities in some regions, and women may be entitled to flexible hours, the ability to work from home, or other forms of support. Employers are obligated to engage in open conversations with employees to assess their needs and provide reasonable adjustments to help them manage their health while continuing to perform their roles.

Beyond legal rights, creating a culture that embraces and respects the natural rhythms of all employees can have a profound impact on job satisfaction, morale, and engagement. By training managers and teams to understand the effects of menstrual cycles, workplaces can reduce stigma, foster empathy, and create a supportive environment where everyone can thrive.

16 Build up your strength

"Take care of your body. It's the only place you have to live." — Jim Rohn

Keep it moving

In many corporate environments, we spend long hours sitting at desks, often without much physical movement or challenge. As a result, it's easy to overlook the importance of physical strength in achieving success and well-being at work. Physical health plays a vital role in maintaining energy, focus, and overall performance, even in jobs that aren't physically demanding on the surface.

It's not about having the perfect physique, being the strongest, or comparing yourself to others in terms of ability, it's about taking the steps to become the healthiest version of yourself. Focus on your well-being and embracing your unique strengths. Physical and mental well-being isn't limited to those who are able-bodied; individuals with disabilities can also thrive by focusing on achieving their personal physical goals. It's about prioritizing what feels right for your body and mind.

In ancient cultures, physical activity wasn't just a choice, it was a matter of survival. Hunting, gathering, and manual labour were the original workouts, shaping strong, resilient bodies long before gyms and fitness trackers existed.

In ancient Greece, the pursuit of physical fitness was elevated to an art form, driven by the demands of warfare and celebrated through the iconic Olympic Games. While most of us today are fortunate enough not to battle for survival or face the trials of war, the instinct to move around and exercise is deeply embedded in our DNA.

Exercise and movement are profound privileges

In a world where countless people are constrained by illness, disability, war or environmental barriers, the ability to move freely and engage in physical activity is a gift. For those of us who can run, stretch, lift, or dance without restriction, it's easy to forget that this freedom is not universal. Exercise allows us to explore our physical potential, maintain our health, and experience the joy of movement, luxuries that remind us to be grateful for our bodies and the opportunities we have to care for them.

Exercise is a celebration of what your body can do, not a punishment for what you ate. This quote is widely attributed to fitness influencer and author Chloe Madeley, who has emphasized a positive and empowering approach to fitness. The focus should remain on strength, health, and capability rather than guilt or shame related to the foods we eat.

Exercise is a happiness hack

A study published in *JAMA Psychiatry* found that regular physical activity can reduce the risk of developing depression, while the Anxiety and Depression Association of America highlighted that exercise can alleviate symptoms of anxiety and depression by up to around 30%. Even a single workout session can lift your mood for hours, and research from *The Lancet Psychiatry* reveals that people who exercise regularly report fewer days of poor mental health each month.

A regular fitness routine can seriously amp up productivity in ways you might not expect. For starters, working out gives you a natural energy boost by getting your blood pumping and oxygen flowing. That extra energy can keep you powering through your day without hitting that dreaded afternoon slump. Plus, exercise sharpens your focus and concentration. Those post-workout endorphins aren't just good for your mood, they also help you think more clearly and stay on top of tasks, so you can get more done in less time.

Stressed? Regular physical activity is a natural stress-buster, reducing those harmful stress hormones and making you feel more relaxed and in control. And if you're looking to spark creativity, exercise is a game-changer. It's been shown that aerobic workouts, in particular, can boost your creative thinking, making it easier to come up with fresh ideas and solve problems.

Lastly, exercise works wonders for your sleep. It helps regulate your sleep patterns, leaving you feeling refreshed and ready to tackle the day ahead. So, whether you're after a mood lift, a productivity boost, or just better sleep, a good workout might be the answer.

Impact on the workplace

The impact of exercise in the workplace has been studied countless times and its benefits have been consistently proven. According to a study by the American College of Sports Medicine, employees who engage in regular physical activity show around a 20% increase in productivity. This is attributed to improved focus, energy, and overall job performance. When it comes to employee illness, research indicates that employees who exercise regularly take fewer sick days compared to those who do not, highlighting the link between physical fitness and reduced absenteeism.

Not only that, according to the *World Health Organization (WHO)*, regular physical activity can reduce the risk of chronic diseases like cardiovascular disease and diabetes by up to 30%. Exercise also has a significant impact on mental health. A study published in the Journal of Occupational Health Psychology found that employees who stay active report greater job satisfaction. It even extends to work-life balance, research shows that employees who exercise are more likely to feel they have a better balance between work and life outside the office.

On the flip side, long hours of sitting can take a serious toll on your body. Prolonged inactivity leads to back pain, neck and shoulder tension, and weak core muscles. Metabolically, it can contribute to weight gain and increase the risk of type 2 diabetes due to reduced calorie burning and poor insulin sensitivity.

So, yes, we get it, exercise is essential. But in our busy, jam-packed lives, how can we realistically fit movement into our daily routines and make it stick? The key is to start small and build habits that work for you, no matter how hectic your schedule is.

Start simply by walking more

If you are going to start with one simple thing, start with walking. Whether you are someone starting anew on your fitness journey, or a long-time gym rat, incorporating more walking into your life has countless benefits. It's a simple workout that has many powerful benefits, and can be incorporated easily into a busy work routine.

It's a highly productive form of exercise as walking is linked with enhanced cognitive function and can reduce the risk of cognitive decline as you age. Walking, especially in nature, has been shown to reduce stress levels, improve mood, and combat symptoms of anxiety and depression. Walking can be done anywhere and at any time, whether it's a leisurely stroll, brisk power walk, or hiking in nature, making it easier to fit into busy schedules.

Consider your daily schedule, are there meetings where you must attend but will not have an active participation? Schedule in a walk. If you have a way to connect from your phone, and just notify your line manager that you will be walking during the meeting. There's nothing unprofessional or inappropriate about balancing active listening and a 15-minute walk.

Don't let yourself feel any worker's guilt, you are benefitting the company in the long run. Plan this out in advance, block it in your calendar, and you'll find you are more likely to incorporate this practice. If you ever need to justify yourself, just refer to all the multitude of studies done that show how multitasking with walking boosts productivity in the workplace:

o A study led by Stanford researchers (in 2014) found that walking can boost creativity. Participants who walked while brainstorming generated more ideas compared to those who were seated. This effect was observed whether walking occurred indoors or outdoors. The study highlighted that walking can enhance divergent thinking, which is crucial for problem-solving and creative tasks during meetings.

o Research from the University of Illinois (in 2008) demonstrated that even short bursts of physical activity, like walking, can improve attention and executive function. This implies that walking during calls might help maintain focus and cognitive performance during virtual meetings.

- A study from Journal of Occupational Health Psychology (2017) found that physical activity, including walking, can help reduce workplace fatigue and improve overall job satisfaction. Employees who incorporate movement into their workday may experience less mental exhaustion and increased engagement.

Take care of your core strength

The modern workplace, with its long hours of sitting, has significantly contributed to a surge in back pain and related issues. Sedentary lifestyles, compounded by poor posture and improperly designed workstations, place undue strain on the spine and surrounding muscles. Prolonged periods of inactivity can weaken core strength, leading to chronic discomfort and even more serious spinal conditions.

Prolonged sitting, especially with poor ergonomic setup, can lead to neck and shoulder pain, often referred to as "tech neck" or "office syndrome," due to muscle strain from holding a static position. To combat these issues, take advantage of the resources available to you. Most workplaces offer Health & Safety support, including desk setup reviews. A proper ergonomic workstation can make a world of difference, so don't overlook this resource.

Equally important is strengthening your core, which acts as the body's natural brace. A strong core not only reduces lower back strain but also improves posture, balance, and stability. It can alleviate tightness in the hips and pelvis caused by extended sitting, leaving you feeling stronger, lighter, and more agile. Deep core exercises target the muscles beneath the surface layers, focusing on those that provide stability, balance, and support to your spine and pelvis.

These muscles include the transverse abdominis, multifidus, pelvic floor, and diaphragm. Unlike surface-level abdominal muscles (like the rectus abdominis, responsible for six-packs), deep core muscles are crucial for maintaining posture, preventing injury, and improving overall body function.

Examples of Deep Core Exercises:

o Plank Variations (Forearm Plank, Side Plank): Focus on maintaining a straight line from head to toe while engaging the core.

o Dead Bug: Lying on your back with arms and legs raised, alternate extending opposite arms and legs while keeping the lower back pressed into the floor.

o Bird Dog: On hands and knees, extend one arm and the opposite leg while keeping the torso stable. Switch sides.

o Pelvic Floor Activation (Kegels): Engage and lift the pelvic floor muscles as if stopping the flow of urine.

o Bridge: Lying on your back with knees bent, lift your hips toward the ceiling, squeezing the glutes and engaging the core.

The Pilates trend

Pilates has surged in popularity, and it's no wonder why! This exercise method is renowned for its transformative impact on core strength and overall wellness. At its heart, Pilates focuses on precision and control, targeting the deep muscles of the abdomen, lower back, and pelvis. This commitment to strengthening the core not only enhances posture and stability but also supports the entire body's alignment and movement efficiency.

According to the Journal of Bodywork and Movement Therapies, a 12-week Pilates program can boost abdominal muscle strength by around 30%, showcasing its core-strengthening prowess.

Regular practice of Pilates helps to sculpt a leaner physique, improve balance, and reduce the risk of injury. Posture improvements are equally notable, with the Physical Therapy Reviews noting around 20% enhancement in postural alignment after 6 weeks of Pilates. For those battling lower back pain, the British Journal of Sports Medicine reveals that Pilates can reduce pain and enhance functional ability.

With these remarkable stats, Pilates proves to be a powerhouse for strengthening the core and enhancing overall well-being.

Incorporate all and any movement

Once you are comfortable with the basics, have good stamina and are taking care of your core strength, you should be levelling up your forms of exercise. Some of the most effective forms of exercise combine strength, endurance, flexibility, and cardiovascular fitness. Even if you don't have access to a gym to incorporate equipment into your weight training or cardio regime, there are many easily accessible forms of exercise.

Here are some very motivating facts that can kick start your training:

o HIIT: HIIT workouts create an Excess Post-Exercise Oxygen Consumption (EPOC) effect, meaning your body continues to burn calories for hours after the workout ends—sometimes up to 48 hours. A typical 20-minute HIIT session can burn more calories than a 45-minute moderate-intensity workout because of the high intensity and fat-burning potential.

o Strength training: For every pound of muscle you gain, your body burns an additional 6-10 calories per day at rest. This is why strength training is essential for long-term fat loss. Lifting weights doesn't just strengthen muscles—it actually strengthens your bones, reducing the risk of osteoporosis, especially in older adults.

o Running: The euphoria some runners experience isn't just in their heads. It's caused by endocannabinoids, chemical compounds in the brain that are similar to the active ingredients in marijuana, making running a natural "high." In Mexico City, authorities have installed treadmills connected to power generators. When people run on them, they generate energy that helps stabilize buildings against earthquakes—a fascinating example of running's practical applications!

o Swimming: Swimming burns more calories than running at the same intensity because water provides 12 to 14 times more resistance than air, forcing your muscles to work harder. Swimmers develop superior lung capacity. Studies have shown that regular swimmers have a higher lung capacity than most other athletes, thanks to the breathing techniques they use during training.

o Cycling: Studies have shown that cycling regularly can lead to a 50% lower risk of depression. The repetitive motion and focus needed can be meditative and help release stress-relieving endorphins.

Movement is secondary only to breathing, without movement it is difficult to efficiently perform any other functions. When we fully embrace the importance of regular movement, it transforms from a task we try to squeeze into our busy schedules to a natural, ingrained part of our daily routine. It's not just an occasional chore; and once we recognize movement as essential, it becomes second nature, flowing effortlessly into our day.

17 Give yourself the right fuel

"Let food be thy medicine and medicine be thy food." — Hippocrates

Nutrition as medicine

Across the globe, countless cultures have cherished food and herbs as nature's pharmacy, drawing on centuries of wisdom to heal and sustain the body. In traditional Chinese medicine, the idea of food as medicine is not just a philosophy but a way of life. Ingredients like ginger, garlic, and goji berries aren't just staples, they're carefully chosen remedies to balance energy (qi) and address ailments. Similarly, Ayurveda, India's ancient wellness system, turns to vibrant spices like turmeric for its anti-inflammatory magic, cumin for digestive health, and fennel for calming the gut, blending flavour with function.

Indigenous communities worldwide have also leaned on their environment's natural bounty for healing. Native American tribes, for example, harnessed the power of echinacea to boost immunity and willow bark to soothe pain, long before modern pharmaceuticals existed. Today, science is catching up with tradition, uncovering the health benefits of antioxidant-packed berries, inflammation-fighting herbs, and nutrient-dense foods.

This timeless wisdom bridges ancient practices and modern knowledge, reminding us that what we eat is a cornerstone of holistic health. Eating well is like giving your body a VIP treatment. You'll have a steady stream of energy that keeps you going without those annoying afternoon crashes, and your mood will lift as your brain gets the nutrients it craves for peak performance. Plus, a diet rich in fruits, veggies, and whole grains keeps your digestive system in check. Your skin will glow, and you'll enjoy more restful nights thanks to improved sleep quality. So, when you nourish your body with the right foods, you're setting yourself up for a life full of vitality and zest.

This chapter is here to inform and inspire, but it's not a substitute for professional nutritional advice. Before making any changes to your diet, do be sure to consult a qualified healthcare expert.

Benefits at work

Healthy eating is so much more than a feel-good habit, it's a transformative tool for workplace morale. The science is both compelling and extensive. For instance, research published in the Journal of Occupational and Environmental Medicine found that employees who maintain a well-balanced diet are around 25% more productive than their counterparts. This isn't just about ticking more items off the to-do list, it's about sharper focus, improved problem-solving, and the stamina to handle challenges with ease.

But the benefits don't stop at productivity. Employees who prioritize nutritious meals typically take fewer sick days, underscoring the link between healthy eating and presence. With fewer colds, fatigue, and chronic illnesses, a healthier workforce is a more present and engaged team. Even more fascinating is the impact on brainpower. According to the Harvard T.H. Chan School of Public Health, a diet rich in fruits, vegetables, and whole grains can enhance cognitive function by as much as around 30%. This means better decision-making, more innovative thinking, and the ability to adapt quickly in high-pressure situations.

Good health isn't just about the physical body, our mental health benefits just as much. Research from the Journal of Clinical Psychiatry shows that a nutrient-rich diet can lower the risk of depression and anxiety by around 20%. In the workplace, this means more resilient employees, stronger collaboration, and a culture of positivity. When people feel good mentally and emotionally, they bring their best selves to work.

For employers, there's a clear financial advantage. Companies that prioritize employee well-being often see a reduction in healthcare costs, thanks to lower risks of chronic illnesses like diabetes and heart disease. Simply put, investing in employee's health isn't just the right thing to do, it's a smart business move with real returns. In essence, healthy eating isn't just a lifestyle choice, it's a strategic advantage. Science confirms it: the road to a healthier, happier, and more productive lifestyle starts on our plate.

Mind gut connection

The mind-gut connection is one of the most extraordinary revelations in modern science, uncovering a dynamic, two-way communication system between our brain and gut that profoundly influences every aspect of our well-being. This interplay, known as the gut-brain axis, is far more than a digestive process, it's a biological dialogue that shapes our emotions, mental health, and cognitive function.

The gut, home to trillions of microbes, is a bustling hub that produces key neurotransmitters, including serotonin the chemical often dubbed the "happiness hormone." Incredibly, about 90% of the body's serotonin is made in the gut, emphasizing how deeply intertwined our digestive health is with our mood and emotional state. This explains why stress and anxiety can trigger digestive issues, but more intriguingly, an unhealthy gut can send the same distress signals back to the brain.

About 70% of our immune system resides in the gut, playing a vital role in mental clarity and emotional resilience. A balanced gut microbiome supports a robust immune system, reducing inflammation that can otherwise contribute to mental fatigue and mood instability. Emerging research even suggests there may be potential links between gut health and conditions like ADHD, autism, and Alzheimer's disease.

Strengthening the gut-brain connection is within our control. Nourishing your gut with a fibre-rich diet filled with fruits, vegetables, fermented foods, and prebiotics feeds the beneficial microbes that keep this system in harmony. Managing stress through mindfulness, meditation, or yoga prevents cortisol from disrupting gut health. And don't underestimate the power of sleep, quality rest allows the gut and brain to reset and recalibrate, improving overall well-being.

One of the most fascinating revelations from the book *The Mind-Gut Connection* is the critical role our gut's microbiome plays in shaping both our mental and physical health. Dr. Emeran Mayer unveils that the gut is quite literally our "second brain." This network of neurons in the gut constantly sends signals to the brain, influencing how we handle stress, regulate our emotions, and make decisions.

Recommended read: The Mind-Gut Connection by Dr. Emeran Mayer.

Focus on source foods

When it comes to the gold standard of nutrition, the key isn't in fad diets or trends but in a lifestyle that embraces balance, variety, and whole, unprocessed foods. Imagine a way of eating that energizes your body, sharpens your mind, protects you from chronic diseases, and potentially adds vibrant, healthy years to your life.

That's the magic of a balanced, nutrient-dense diet inspired by nature's finest offerings. At the heart of this approach is a plant-based focus, a vibrant array of fruits, vegetables, legumes, and whole grains forming the cornerstone of every meal. These foods aren't just colourful; they're nutritional powerhouses packed with essential vitamins, minerals, antioxidants, and fibre. An don't underestimate the power of small but mighty additions like nuts and seeds.

The benefits are extraordinary; they combat inflammation, support healthy digestion, and help prevent diseases like diabetes, heart disease, and even certain cancers. A Harvard study found that individuals who consumed at least five servings of fruits and vegetables daily had around 30% lower risk of premature death than those who didn't. That's a plate full of life-saving potential.

Embracing a plant-based focus doesn't mean cutting out animal products, though many vegetarians and vegans thrive equally without them. Meat, poultry, and fish are highly nutritious and can play a vital role in certain balanced diets, offering essential nutrients like protein, iron, zinc, and omega-3 fatty acids. The key lies in variety and balance. A plant-based approach simply emphasizes making fruits, vegetables, whole grains, and legumes the star of your meals, with any animal products playing a supporting role.

This approach is backed by global longevity studies, particularly from Blue Zones, regions renowned for their high numbers of centenarians (people living over 100 years).

These areas reveal that diets rich in plants, with moderate amounts of meat or fish, are linked to longer, healthier lives. Take Okinawa, Japan, where about 80% of their diet is plant-based, with only small portions of fish or meat.

This balance contributes to some of the lowest rates of chronic disease in the world, proving that moderation and variety are key to living a long, vibrant life. Whether you're savouring roasted vegetables alongside grilled chicken or topping a fresh salad with a perfectly seared piece of salmon, this plant-forward approach encourages balance without feeling restricted. It's about filling your plate with a colourful variety of nourishing foods, all while enjoying the flavours you love.

By choosing fresh, whole foods and staying mindful of your choices, you're not just fuelling your body; you're cultivating a relationship with food that enhances every aspect of your life. It's a delicious, rewarding journey that leads to lasting well-being, one bite at a time.

Understanding macros

The three main macronutrients; carbohydrates, proteins, and fats, form the foundation of any diet, each playing a unique and essential role in fuelling and maintaining the body. Carbohydrates are the body's primary energy source, breaking down into glucose to power your brain and muscles; they're found in foods like grains, fruits, and vegetables.

Proteins are the building blocks for repair and growth, supporting muscle maintenance, immune function, and enzyme production; they're abundant in meat, fish, legumes, and dairy.

Fats, often misunderstood, are vital for hormone production, nutrient absorption, and long-term energy; healthy sources include avocados, nuts, seeds, and olive oil. Healthy fats, like those from fatty fish such as salmon and sardines, are the premium fuel for your brain, fortifying your heart and sharpening your mind. They help balance cholesterol, quell inflammation, and safeguard against cognitive decline.

A truly balanced diet involves nourishing your body with the right proportions of macronutrients tailored to your needs. When one of these macronutrients is overrepresented or lacking, your body's equilibrium is disrupted. For instance, consuming too many refined carbs can lead to quick energy surges followed by sharp crashes, contributing to weight gain and increasing your risk of type 2 diabetes.

On the flip side, excessive protein can overload the kidneys and dehydrate the body, while too much unhealthy fat, can raise cholesterol and heighten your risk of heart disease. Achieving the right balance ensures steady energy, better overall health, and smoother body function. It's important to remember that not all carbs, proteins, and fats are created equal.

Quality matters just as much as quantity. Complex carbs, like whole grains, fruits, and vegetables, provide a sustained energy source and essential nutrients, while refined carbs can cause rapid energy dips and promote weight gain.

Lean proteins, such as chicken, fish, beans, and tofu, are excellent for muscle recovery without unnecessary saturated fats, while processed meats come with added health risks. Healthy fats from avocados, nuts, seeds, and olive oil support brain function and heart health, whereas trans fats and excess saturated fats fuel inflammation and chronic conditions. Choosing nutrient-dense options within each macro category is the key to unlocking your body's full potential.

Not all calories are used by our bodies in the same way. Nutrient-dense foods, like whole grains, lean proteins, and healthy fats, are absorbed efficiently, fuelling your body with sustained energy and supporting essential functions. On the other hand, calories from processed snacks or sugary treats are too quickly absorbed, spiking your blood sugar and encouraging fat storage.

Though they may provide the same caloric content, "empty calories" lack the nutrients your body needs to thrive. Focusing on the quality of what you eat is far more important than simply just counting calories.

Take your full lunch break hour!

Eating at your desk might seem like a productivity hack, but it can do more harm than good. When we eat while working, we tend to rush through meals, which can lead to poor digestion. Studies show that eating too quickly makes it harder for the body to signal fullness, often leading to overeating and discomfort.

On the mental side, trying to juggle work and meals can distract your brain from both tasks, reducing your focus and enjoyment. In fact, constantly eating at your desk can even ramp up stress levels. Research from the UK's Office for National Statistics found that employees who take regular lunch breaks have lower stress levels and report higher job satisfaction. In fact, those who take a full break return to work feeling more energized and focused.

Incorporating a full lunch hour away from your desk isn't just a break, it actively improves your productivity rather than hinder it.

Simple recipes and meal planning

We all understand the importance of eating well and maintaining a balanced diet. Yet, with hectic work schedules and constant demands on our time, finding the moments to craft a balanced meal can feel like a juggling act. So, how best can you streamline your meal planning to effortlessly blend nutrition and convenience?

o Simplify with smart planning: Instead of overcomplicating your meals, focus on simplicity. Choose a few versatile, nutritious recipes that can be easily prepared and adapted. Think of dishes that work as leftovers or can be reinvented into new meals. This will save you time and effort throughout the week.

o Batch cook like a pro: Set aside a block of time, perhaps on a quieter weekend day, to cook in bulk. Prepare large portions of grains, proteins, and vegetables. Store them in the fridge or freezer in individual servings. This way, you can quickly assemble meals with minimal daily effort.

o Embrace quick and easy recipes: Incorporate recipes that are ready in 15 minutes or less. One-pot meals, stir-fries, and sheet pan dishes are not only efficient but also packed with flavour and nutrition. They're perfect for those nights when time is of the essence.

o Fill up your freezer: Stock your freezer with pre-portioned meals and ingredients. Soups, stews, and casseroles freeze beautifully and can be lifesavers on particularly busy days. Having a variety of frozen options ensures you always have a healthy choice at hand.

o   Keep a pantry of essentials: Fill your pantry with staple items like canned beans, pasta, rice, and frozen vegetables. These staples can quickly transform into nourishing meals, saving you time on grocery runs and meal prep.

o   Stick to a simple grocery list: Create a focused shopping list based on your meal plan. Sticking to this list not only ensures you get the ingredients you need but also helps you avoid impulse buys, keeping your meal planning efficient and on track.

Master the Meal Grid

A meal grid is a structured way to visualise meals, helping ensure that you're getting a balanced intake of nutrients across the day. Create a weekly meal grid to streamline your choices. Outline your breakfast, lunch, and dinner options, utilizing the ingredients from your shopping list. This visual guide helps you make quick decisions, eliminating the stress of daily meal planning.

Planning an entire week of meals can feel overwhelming, so start small by focusing on just the first three days. Creating a simple, healthy meal plan for the beginning of the week can set the tone and give you the energy you need to tackle whatever comes your way.

Example of a balanced meal-grid:

Day	Meal	Protein	Carbs	Healthy Fats	Veggies/ Fruits
Mon	Break-fast	Scrambled eggs	Toast	Avocado	Spinach
	Lunch	Grilled chicken	Quinoa	Olive oil	Mixed greens, tomatoes
	Snacks	Greek yogurt	Granola	Almonds	Apple slices
	Dinner	Baked salmon	Sweet potato	Coconut oil	Broccoli
Tues	Break-fast	Greek yoghurt	Overnight oats	Walnuts	Berries
	Lunch	Egg omelette	Dices potatoes	Olive oil	Bell peppers
	Snacks	Peanut butter	Rye crackers	Peanut butter	Banana
	Dinner	Grilled Chicken	Black beans, rice	Avocado	Kale, sweetcorn
Wed	Break-fast	Smoked salmon	Bagel	Cream cheese	Cucumber slices
	Lunch	Sliced turkey	Wholegrain wrap	Avocado	Lettuce, tomato
	Snacks	Boiled egg	Chickpea hummus	Olive oil	Carrot Slices
	Dinner	Ground beef	Rice, herbs	Sesame oil	Spring onion, limes

A balanced meal-grid gives you a big-picture overview of your meals, ensuring variety and hitting all the essential food groups. It's flexible, visual, and easy to follow. The beauty of it lies in its simplicity: foods often serve double duty, like veggies acting as both complex carbs and fibre sources, or peanut butter providing protein and healthy fats.

18 Rest, rest and rest some more!

"Sleep is the best meditation." – Dalai Lama

In a society that constantly urges us to stay busy and productive, this quote reminds us that sleep isn't just for recharging, it's a powerful form of self-care. Like meditation, rest allows us to unplug, unwind, and reset. It's the one time when the mind and body can escape the chaos, process the day's emotions, and restore balance.

Throughout history, people have fought for the right to rest. In ancient times, holidays were tied to religious festivals, offering brief escapes from labour. The Industrial Revolution stripped many of these breaks away, leading workers to demand fair hours, weekends, and paid time off. Their struggles shaped the rights we enjoy today, yet in our fast-paced world, we often forget to truly embrace rest. Holidays and time off weren't just given to us; they were won. So, make the most of them, you've earned it.

Take your time-off!

If there's one golden rule for avoiding burnout and maintaining a healthy work-life balance, it's this: guard your time off fiercely.

Taking breaks isn't just about vacations or lounging on a beach, it's about giving your mind and body the reset they need to function at their best. Time away from work allows you to step back from the daily grind, recharge your energy, and gain fresh perspectives. Rest isn't a luxury; it's a necessity for long-term success and well-being.

Even if you're not traveling, scheduling regular time off helps prevent exhaustion and keeps you performing at your peak. And when you're off, truly be off. That means no emails, no calls, and no "just a quick check-in" (unless actual lives are at stake—and no, sending that file to Sandra from accounting doesn't count!). Your downtime is sacred, and treating it as such keeps you sharp, focused, and ready to tackle new challenges.

No emails, no calls, no "just a quick check-in", unless you're genuinely in a job where actual lives are on the line (and no, sending that file to accounting doesn't qualify as saving lives!). Your downtime is sacred, and treating it as such is key to staying energized, clear-headed, and ready to tackle whatever work throws your way.

The connection between rest and workplace performance is undeniable. A Harvard Business Review study found that employees who take regular vacations are 40% more likely to receive a raise or promotion than those who skip them. Why? Because well-rested professionals return with renewed energy, sharper problem-solving skills, and greater creativity, key ingredients for high performance.

Time off also reduces stress and prevents burnout, leading to fewer sick days, higher engagement, and stronger leadership potential. Companies that encourage employees to take their paid time off often see a boost in workplace morale, collaboration, and retention. When people are well-rested, they're more motivated, productive, and effective in their roles, benefitting both individuals and the organization as a whole. S

So, set that boundary, take your breaks, and come back stronger. Your career (and your sanity) will thank you.

The optimal balance

Finding the right balance of time off is all about managing your workload, stress levels, and personal needs. Instead of saving all your vacation days for one long break, consider taking multiple shorter vacations (3–5 days) throughout the year. Research shows that frequent breaks are more effective at preventing burnout and maintaining productivity than a single extended holiday.

Seasonal shifts can also impact your energy levels, winter fatigue and summer restlessness are common. Planning time off during these natural dips can help you recharge when you need it most. Likewise, scheduling breaks after major projects or during slower work periods ensures you're not overwhelmed before or after your time away, allowing you to fully enjoy your rest.

By spreading out your time off strategically, you create a rhythm of recovery that keeps you energized, focused, and performing at your best all year long.

Sleep away all of your problems

Well-rested employees can completely transform a workplace. When people get the sleep they need, they show up sharper, more focused, and ready to tackle challenges with creativity and energy. With lower stress levels and a reduced risk of burnout, they're not only more productive but also happier and healthier, boosting morale across the entire team.

Sleep isn't just about feeling rested, it's essential for long-term health. In fact, the glymphatic system, a crucial brain-cleaning process discovered in 2012, clears out toxic waste notably while we rest. It becomes most active during deep sleep, flushing out toxins, dead cells, and beta-amyloid proteins, the same proteins linked to Alzheimer's and other neurodegenerative diseases.

Without deep sleep, this waste builds up, increasing the risk of cognitive decline over time. During deep sleep, the body releases human growth hormone (HGH), which is essential for muscle repair, tissue growth, and overall recovery. Athletes and active individuals who prioritize sleep see faster healing, improved endurance, and better physical performance.

Getting a good night's sleep is something we can actively improve with the right habits. From creating a relaxing bedtime routine to managing stress and optimizing our sleep environment, there are plenty of proactive steps we can take to enhance sleep quality. Small changes, like reducing screen time before bed, can make a big difference in how rested and refreshed we feel each day.

o   Establishing a consistent sleep schedule by going to bed and waking up at the same time each day helps regulate the body's circadian rhythm.

o   Creating a relaxing bedtime routine, such as reading, taking a warm bath, or practicing mindfulness, signals the brain that it's time to wind down.

o   Limiting blue light exposure from screens at least an hour before bed prevents disruptions in melatonin production, the hormone responsible for sleep.

o   Optimizing the sleep environment, keeping the room cool, dark, and quiet, enhances sleep quality, while investing in a comfortable mattress and pillows supports better posture and reduces night-time discomfort.

o   Additionally, be mindful of caffeine intake, avoiding stimulants in the afternoon and opting for calming herbal teas or magnesium-rich foods to promote relaxation.

Women need even more sleep

The eight-hour workday was born out of fierce labour movements in the late 19th and early 20th centuries, a direct response to the gruelling, inhumane hours of the Industrial Revolution. Workers, exhausted by the backbreaking demands of the Industrial Revolution, rallied behind the slogan: "Eight hours for work, eight hours for rest, and eight hours for what we will". While the eight hours of rest aligns with research on optimal sleep duration, there's a glaring problem. Much of that research historically centred on the male body, leaving women's biological needs overlooked.

Recent research is shedding light on the unique sleep needs of women, revealing that the female body often requires notably more sleep. Some studies suggest women may benefit from 9 to 10 hours of sleep each night to fully recharge. Women's brains work hard, constantly multitasking and problem-solving, which increases the need for deeper recovery. Yet many of us have to settle for the standard 7–8 hours, a benchmark based on the male body, all while juggling demanding work schedules and personal responsibilities.

For women, quality sleep is more critical, as it directly impacts both physical and mental health. Sleep helps regulate key hormones like cortisol and oestrogen, which influence stress levels, metabolism, and reproductive health. It also plays a major role in brain function, reducing the risk of anxiety and depression, conditions women are more susceptible to due to hormonal fluctuations. To make matters worse, women are more prone to sleep disorders like insomnia, and chronic sleep deprivation adds to their long-term risks of burnout and health issues.

This imbalance in sleep is impacted even further by work practices of being constantly available, particularly as both men and women often work beyond their scheduled hours, further eating into precious downtime. For women, the stakes are even higher, underscoring the urgent need to address the unique challenges they face in achieving work-life-sleep balance.

Rest is a priority above all else

As a personal anecdote, I once had the good fortune to work alongside a lovely, kind colleague who was the epitome of dedication. However, she was always working tirelessly around the clock and sacrificing her personal time for the sake of her career. She put off experiences, holidays, and moments of rest, in order to meet deadlines and close out critical projects. Then, one day, the unthinkable happened. Our team were utterly shocked to learn that she had passed away unexpectedly, due to unforeseen health issues. It was a stark and painful reminder: no job is worth sacrificing your health and well-being. This experience taught me a profound lesson, while it's important to be committed to your career, it's equally important to protect your health, enjoy your life, and find balance.

At the end of the day, we are replaceable at work, but to our loved ones we are irreplaceable.

19 Grow your investments

"Investing in yourself is the best investment you will ever make. It will not only improve your life, but it will also improve the lives of all those around you."

– Robin Sharma

Making smart choices

This chapter is not financial advice, but rather a foundation of knowledge intended to help you conduct your own research and seek professional financial guidance for to your specific situation.

Although this chapter encourages ways you can improve your financial health, investing isn't just about money, it's about you. It's about pouring time and energy into feeling good now, healing from the past, and laying the groundwork for a future you'll be proud of. Too often, we're conditioned to think of investing solely in terms of finances, tied to strict budgets and future goals, while sacrificing the beauty and richness of the present moment. It is easy to fall into that trap, chasing financial discipline at the expense of life's experiences.

But here's the truth: money, at its core, is simply a tool, a flow of energy and resources. It's not about hoarding or spending recklessly; it's about balance. Use it to create a life that feels abundant now and sets you up for the future you deserve.

Making smart choices with your money starts with understanding your core values. When you take the time to truly know yourself, beyond the noise of ads, social media, and societal expectations—you discover what genuinely lights you up. What hobbies, interests, and goals are authentically you, and not just a product of external influences? By aligning your spending with your true self, you can create a life that feels both fulfilling and purpose-driven.

We see it all around us, people breaking the mould to live life on their own terms. Some ditch the 9-to-5 grind to travel the globe and thrive as freelancers. Others are home bodies, starting families early and building lives centred around their loved ones. Then there are the trailblazers, so deeply passionate about their craft that they rise to become world-renowned experts. And let's not forget the selfless souls who dedicate their lives to caring for others, answering the call to save lives and make the world a better place. These stories remind us that there's no single "right" path. Each of these spend their income in entirely different ways, but their spending habits support their pursuit of each of their individual paths.

It can be difficult to identify ways in which you could invest in yourself, so I've put together some suggestions grouped by topics that are often coupled when it comes to balancing overall wellness:

Education and skills	Physical & Mental Health	Emotional connection & resilience	Purpose and meaning
Take courses or workshops	Regular exercise outdoors or at home	Schedule in set quality time with family or friends	Travel to broaden your horizons and explore new activities
Puck up a new hobby or skills that spark joy	A gym pass to a gym that excites you	Get a mentor at work who uplifts you	Volunteer in your community
Invest in certification that boost your career	Enjoy high quality and nourishing foods	Set a challenge like running a marathon	Organize group outings
Learn a new language	Practice meditation or journaling	Keep a self-reflection or gratitude diary	Offer to mentor others
Attend networking events in your field	Invest in therapy or counselling	Identify stress triggers and work to reduce	Regularly set and check-in with your goals

Investing your finances

Investing is more than just crunching numbers, it's the key to unlocking your financial freedom and designing the life you want. For women, it's a game-changer, especially when you consider the unique financial hurdles many of us face: the gender pay gap, career breaks, and the fact that we tend to live longer. Investing flips the script, whether it's building a dream retirement, funding big adventures, or simply growing your wealth, investing gives you the power to take control of your future and create a life that's rich in every sense of the word.

Investing is where the magic happens, but it all starts with saving. Before you can dive into stocks, real estate, or any wealth-building strategy, you need to set the stage by saving a chunk of your income. By consistently putting money aside, you're not just preparing for the future; you're giving yourself the freedom to invest when the right opportunities come along. It's about building a habit that turns small savings into big wins over time. The earlier you start, the sooner you'll be setting the foundation for lasting financial success.

Balancing a budget while still enjoying life is all about finding harmony between financial responsibility and personal fulfilment. It's important to be mindful of saving and managing expenses, but that doesn't mean sacrificing the things that bring you joy. Budgeting is about prioritizing what truly matters, whether it's experiences, hobbies, or treating yourself to something special.

By creating a financial plan that covers essentials and long-term goals, you can give yourself the freedom to spend on what enriches your life without guilt. The key is smart, intentional spending that aligns with your values and lets you enjoy the present while securing your future.

Be mindful of lifestyle inflation

In today's world, we're surrounded by high earners who seem to have it all, but scratch the surface, and you'll find they often own very little outright in their name. Those hefty pay checks and jaw-dropping bonuses vanish as quickly as they come, funnelled into extravagant dinners, endless champagne toasts, and oversized mansions with equally massive mortgages. From the outside, it all looks dazzling. But behind the scenes, the sparkle fades quickly.

Debt quietly accumulates, retirement drifts further out of reach, and their entire lifestyle balances on a knife's edge, one economic downturn or unexpected job loss away from collapse. Life has a way of throwing curveballs when you least expect it. Without a solid financial plan or disciplined budgeting, even the wealthiest can find themselves treading water. True wealth isn't measured by how much you earn; it's about how thoughtfully and strategically you manage what you have.

A personal anecdote and powerful life lesson I observed, was the downfall of an executive who had once been working in the glamorous investment banking roles of the

1990s. Back then, these bankers were the stars of the financial world, orchestrating massive deals, IPOs, and mergers with gruelling hours and high-stakes decisions. They were the beating heart of banking, earning six-figure bonuses and basking in a lifestyle of indulgence.

But the tides of time spared no one. As the financial industry evolved, their once-glamorous roles began to fade into obsolescence. Technology, with its relentless march, introduced AI, algorithmic trading, and automation, streamlining tasks that once required human grit. Meanwhile, the aftermath of the 2008 financial crisis ushered in stricter regulations, curbing high-risk practices and redirecting the industry's focus toward fintech innovation and decentralized finance.

For many of these once-mighty bankers, the shift wasn't just a career transition, it was a brutal wake-up call. Accustomed to the excesses of wealth, they suddenly found themselves unprepared for a world that had outpaced their skill sets. The fast-growing realms of fintech, data analytics, and AI left them scrambling to keep up. For some, early retirement wasn't a choice, it was the only option.

Careers that had once seemed unshakable became relics of a bygone era. Without the technical expertise or flexibility to transition into emerging roles, these once-high earners faced diminishing opportunities. Many had to downsize their lives, relying on savings (or grappling with the consequences of overspending) as their once-lucrative careers became relics of a bygone era.

This individual was once earning such high bonuses, that they could have easily retired at 40. However, having lived above their means for many years, found themselves in pursuit of new career paths in their 60s. If only they had tackled their finances with a bit more foresight, planning for the day when their sky-high incomes might nosedive, they could have enjoyed a long and early retirement. They passed up a golden opportunity to build a foundation of lasting financial security.

Saving and investing – start as soon as you can

Saving and investing are privileges not everyone can afford. If you're fortunate enough to have money left over after covering all your essential bills and expenses, consider it a gift, and use it wisely. The smartest move you can make is to set boundaries for your lifestyle spending and channel the rest into investments that grow your future.

Saving is the act of setting aside money for future use, typically in a low-risk, easily accessible account, like a savings account or a money market account. The primary goal of saving is to preserve your money and ensure it's available when you need it, whether it's for an emergency fund, a big purchase, or short-term goals like a vacation or a down payment on a house. While savings accounts offer safety, they often provide lower returns, especially when factoring in inflation.

Investing, on the other hand, involves putting your money into assets like stocks, bonds, real estate, or mutual funds, with the expectation that it will grow over time. Unlike saving, investing comes with higher risk because the value of your investments can rise and fall depending on market conditions. However, investing offers the potential for higher returns, which is why it's generally used to build wealth over the long term.

People typically invest for goals like retirement or funding education, where they have years or decades to ride out market fluctuations. Even if you are just saving into a standard savings account, make sure that you are considering the best interest rates possible and frequently review your options across lenders. Investments gather momentum and grow exponentially.

The magic behind this growth is compound interest. Essentially, when you invest, you're not just earning returns on your initial investment, but also on the gains that accumulate over time. It's a cycle that accelerates as your wealth grows. Imagine you invest $1,000 and earn a 5% return in the first year. You now have $1,050, and in the second year, you earn 5% on the full $1,050, not just the original $1,000. Over time, this compounding effect can lead to impressive growth.

The longer your money has to grow, the more powerful compounding becomes, turning even modest investments into substantial wealth over the years.

This is why starting early with investments is one of the smartest financial moves you can make. Ultimately, both are important in a healthy financial strategy, saving gives you security and liquidity, while investing helps you build wealth over time.

Leverage budgeting apps

Budgeting apps take the hassle out of tracking your finances, turning what used to be a tedious task into a seamless experience. By connecting directly to your bank accounts and credit cards, these apps automatically log your income and expenses, eliminating the need for manual calculations and ensuring pinpoint accuracy.

But that's just the start. Budget apps categorize your spending—whether it's groceries, dining out, utilities, or entertainment—so you can see exactly where your money goes. This clarity makes it much easier to pinpoint areas where you can cut back or redirect funds to what matters most. What's more, these apps are incredibly flexible. They allow you to create customized budgets tailored to your unique financial situation and adjust them as your needs or goals change.

Create your own tracker

Even if you prefer the hands-on approach of manually creating your budget—whether it's jotting it down in a notebook or organizing it in an Excel spreadsheet—you're already taking a powerful step toward financial control. By actively reviewing your income and expenses, you're not only identifying areas of excess spending but also opening the door to smarter financial decisions.

Research shows that people who write down their budgets, even manually, are more likely to stick to them because the act of recording enhances awareness and accountability. Excel, in particular, offers flexibility with built-in formulas, charts, and pivot tables to visualize spending trends and simulate financial scenarios.

Manual budgeting may take more effort, but it gives you an intimate understanding of your finances, allowing you to spot patterns and redirect money toward savings, investments, or other meaningful goals. Every cell you fill or line you write is a step closer to financial clarity and success.

Automate your savings

Automating your savings is like putting your financial goals on autopilot, it eliminates the temptation to spend before you save. Studies show that people are more likely to save consistently when the process is automatic, because it takes willpower out of the equation.

Set up automatic transfers from your checking account to a savings or investment account as soon as your pay check hits. By doing this, you're "paying yourself first," a proven strategy for building wealth. Treat your savings as if it were a mandatory.

Mental models for saving

A general approach can be the '50/30/20 rule', as a simple, yet effective budgeting method that helps you manage your money by dividing your after-tax income into three main categories: needs, wants, and savings or debt repayment. The percentages can be adjusted based on your income, location, or personal goals. For instance, in a high-cost-of-living area, your "needs" category might temporarily take up more than 50%.

A lot of people refer to the 50/30/20 rule which considers:

- o 50% of your income for needs (rent, utilities, groceries).
- o 30% for wants (entertainment, dining out).
- o 20% for savings and debt repayment.

Wants are non-essential expenses that enhance your lifestyle and provide enjoyment. This category ensures you don't feel deprived while saving. Budgeting for wants allows you to enjoy life in moderation without compromising your financial goals.

For some, a more personalized approach to budgeting can make all the difference. Start by carefully reviewing your monthly expenses and identifying what's truly a "must-have." Everything outside of that category can be treated as an extra. Once you've established your essential costs, you can then decide how much of your remaining income will go toward savings, leaving a set amount for discretionary spending, like dining out, entertainment, or little indulgences. Everyone's goals and needs are different, so this flexible system allows you to allocate funds in a way that aligns with what matters most to you.

Decipher your income and taxes

It's easy to be drawn in by a high total compensation when considering a new job, but the key is understanding how this breakdown into the various elements of compensation and then ultimately into your net pay, the actual amount that ends up in your bank account. Companies often promote "total compensation" figures that sound impressive but may include bonuses and other perks that don't immediately translate into take-home pay.

It's essential to break down how the pay is structured and calculate your true take-home amount. Gross pay Is the total amount you earn before deductions, encompassing your base salary, bonuses, overtime, and any other income your employer agrees to pay.

However, the number that truly matters is your net pay, the amount that actually lands in your bank account after deductions like taxes, health insurance, retirement contributions, and other withholdings.

But your total salary package extends far beyond just your base pay. Many companies offer performance bonuses that reward your hard work, along with sign-on or retention bonuses to keep you on board. In high-growth environments like start-ups or executive roles, stock options and equity are often the game-changers. Plus, profit-sharing allows you to tap into the company's success, offering an additional boost to your overall compensation.

Retirement benefits are essential for securing long-term financial stability, and many corporate roles offer pension plans, such as 401(k)s in the U.S., often with employer-matching contributions. These plans allow women to steadily build their retirement savings over time. In the UK, employers typically match pension contributions, offering a strong foundation for financial growth. A well-structured pension plan can help close the retirement savings gap, particularly for women who might experience career breaks or live longer than men.

Each component of a salary package can be taxed differently, depending on the type of compensation and each country's local tax laws. Here's how tax rates may vary for different elements of a total salary package:

o Base Salary: This is usually subject to ordinary income tax rates, which are progressive—meaning the more you earn, the higher percentage of your income is taxed. In many countries, this ranges from 10% to over 40%, depending on income brackets.

o Bonuses: In most cases, bonuses are taxed as regular income, so they're subject to the same tax rates as your base salary. However, in some places, they might be subject to supplemental tax rates, which can range from 22% to 37% in the U.S., for example.

o Stock Options: Taxation depends on whether they are incentive stock options (ISOs) or non-qualified stock options (NSOs). ISOs may qualify for capital gains tax if you meet specific holding requirements, while NSOs are taxed as ordinary income when exercised. Capital gains tax is often lower than income tax, typically around 15%-20%, depending on how long you hold the stock for.

o RSUs: These are taxed as ordinary income when they vest, meaning you pay income tax, at your local rate, on the value of the shares at the time they're granted.

o Profit-Sharing: Profit-sharing payments are taxed as ordinary income, but they might also be eligible for certain tax-deferred benefits if they are contributed to a retirement plan. In that case, you wouldn't be taxed until you withdraw the funds.

Higher taxes on certain parts of your salary package can quickly turn an attractive compensation offer into less than you'd expect. While the total figure might look impressive on paper, the reality is that once taxes kick in, whether it's on bonuses, stock options, or other perks, the take-home pay could end up being only marginally higher than what you're earning now. It's crucial to dig into the details and consider the tax impact before getting swept away by a big-sounding offer.

Investment opportunities

The everyday investor has a world of opportunities to grow their wealth, ranging from high-risk ventures with thrilling potential to steady, low-risk options that provide peace of mind. For those seeking simplicity, high-yield savings accounts and certificates of deposit provide safe, low-risk options. Stocks offer ownership in companies and the potential for high returns, while bonds provide a steadier income stream with lower risk.

Mutual funds and ETFs (exchange-traded funds) allow individuals to diversify their portfolios without picking individual assets, making them ideal for beginners. Real estate, whether through purchasing property or investing in REITs (real estate investment trusts), offers tangible assets and long-term growth potential.

Now, newer trends like cryptocurrency and peer-to-peer lending platforms have opened alternative investment avenues for those willing to explore innovative markets. Cryptocurrencies like Bitcoin and Ethereum have seen explosive growth since their inception, with Bitcoin's value skyrocketing from mere cents in 2009 to tens of thousands of dollars today.

Beyond traditional crypto, blockchain applications are expanding their reach, unlocking new possibilities in finance, supply chains, and even real estate. These emerging trends represent exciting frontiers for investors, offering the potential for transformative returns while shaping the future of global industries.

Diversifying investments is crucial for managing risk and ensuring steady returns, as it reduces reliance on the performance of any single asset. By spreading your portfolio across different asset classes, like stocks, bonds, real estate, and alternative investments, you protect yourself from the wild swings of any single market.

During the 2008 financial crisis, investors heavily focused on stocks suffered deep losses, while those who had allocated funds to bonds or commodities like gold weathered the storm more effectively. Fast forward to 2020, as the pandemic crushed tourism stocks, tech and healthcare sectors surged, proving the power of a balanced approach. The performance of investments over the last 20 years has varied significantly across asset classes, driven by economic cycles, technological innovation, and global events.

Stocks have generally performed well, with major indices like the S&P 500 showing average annual returns of around 9-10%. Tech stocks, particularly giants like Apple, Amazon, and Microsoft, have been standout performers, driving much of the growth in the last two decades. Bonds, especially U.S. Treasury bonds, have provided steady, lower-risk returns. While not as high as stocks, they played a crucial role during economic downturns like the 2008 financial crisis and the COVID-19 pandemic, offering stability.

Bonds, stocks and funds explained

Bonds, stocks, and funds are the building blocks of investing, each with its unique role and appeal. Bonds are like a loan you give to a government or company in exchange for regular interest payments and the promise of getting your money back at maturity, making them a steady, low-risk option. Stocks, on the other hand, let you own a piece of a company, giving you a stake in its success (or failure). They offer higher growth potential but with more ups and downs.

Funds, such as mutual funds or ETFs, are the ultimate team players, they pool money from many investors to buy a mix of stocks, bonds, or other assets, offering built-in diversification and professional management. While bonds are for stability and stocks for growth, funds strike a balance, making them an ideal choice for investors who want variety without picking individual investments.

Understanding these differences helps you build a portfolio that fits your goals and risk tolerance.

Recommended read: Girls that invest by Simran Kaur

The power of property

The property market, spanning both residential and non-residential sectors, has long been a powerhouse for wealth creation, consistently rewarding landlords with impressive returns through rental income and asset appreciation. Residential real estate in particular has seen tremendous growth, with global property values more than doubling in many regions.

For example, in the U.S., the median home price rose from approximately $150,000 in 2003 to over $400,000 in 2023, fuelled by low-interest rates and urban demand. The twin forces of urbanization and population growth have spiked demand for housing, driving up property values and rental rates. From cosy suburban homes to bustling city apartments, landlords benefit as housing shortages keep rents on an upward trajectory.

On the commercial side, properties like office spaces, retail outlets, and industrial warehouses have become increasingly valuable, bolstered by economic growth and shifting business trends. The e-commerce revolution, in particular, has turned logistics hubs and warehouses into goldmines for investors.

Meanwhile, the rise of mixed-use developments and co-working spaces offers landlords new opportunities to thrive in a dynamic market. Together, these trends highlight real estate's enduring status as a versatile and profitable investment avenue, combining stability with growth potential.

Looking ahead, some forecasts predict continued growth, though at a more moderate pace. Some analysts project a shift toward sustainability-focused properties and urban regeneration projects as key trends. Emerging markets are also expected to offer lucrative opportunities. While rising interest rates and inflation could pose challenges, property investments are anticipated to remain resilient, buoyed by population growth and increasing demand for urban infrastructure.

Recommended read: Essential Property Investment Calculations by Robert Heaton

Private equity and angel investing

The most rewarding business venture is often the one you build from the ground up, where you have full control over its direction and success. But if starting your own business isn't on the cards, the next best opportunity is joining forces with innovative founders in the early stages of their journey. This is where private equity comes in, a world brimming with potential for those who have an eye for promising ideas and the drive to back visionary entrepreneurs.

By investing in early-stage businesses, you can play a pivotal role in helping them thrive, while positioning yourself to reap the rewards of their growth.

Private equity is like the behind-the-scenes engine that powers some of the world's most successful companies. It involves investing in privately owned businesses, those not listed on the stock market, with the goal of enhancing their growth, profitability, and value over time. Private equity firms or investors typically provide capital to help companies expand, restructure, or innovate, often taking an active role in shaping the business.

Angel investing is an exciting gateway into the world of early-stage business private equity, where individuals with capital take on the role of champions for innovative start-ups. These "angel investors" provide funding to entrepreneurs in exchange for equity, betting on the next big idea before it becomes a household name. It's high-risk, high-reward: while many ventures may falter, the ones that succeed can yield extraordinary returns—think early backers of companies like Airbnb or Uber.

Beyond financial gain, angel investing offers the chance to support ground-breaking innovations and build relationships with visionary founders. The opportunities are vast, spanning tech start-ups, sustainable energy solutions, healthcare innovations, and consumer products.

With platforms like AngelList and Seedrs making it easier to discover promising ventures, angel investing has never been more accessible to those looking to combine profit with purpose, shaping the businesses of tomorrow.

Recommended read: The Private Equity Playbook by Adam E. Coffey

20 Postface

As we reach the end, I hope these chapters have offered you both insight and inspiration. From exploring the resilience and contributions of women throughout history to navigating the complexities of modern workplaces. This book is a testament to our power of reflection, growth, and self-discovery. We've delved into strategies for overcoming barriers, finding meaning in your work, and designing a life that aligns with your core values.

Whether you're building a network, honing your health, mastering productivity, or investing in your finances, every step is a step toward empowerment. Remember, progress doesn't happen overnight, but with each decision rooted in purpose, you're crafting a work-life balance that you can truly enjoy.

The future is yours to design, so lead with gratitude, invest in yourself, and boldly pursue your dream life!

Printed in Great Britain
by Amazon